Coaching Tips

How to Become a Successful Coach in any Sport

by Coach Dale L. Tryon

Printed by Sigler Printing & Publishing, Inc.
Ames, Iowa 50010-0887

Library of Congress Catalog Card Number 96-092627
ISBN Number 1-888223-04-9

About the Author

Dale is from a large family of 10 children. The parents are Clarence and Dorothy Tryon of Glidden, Iowa. There are 8 boys and 2 girls in the family. Ray was the oldest, followed by Bill, Dale, Gaylord, Larry, Jerry, Donna, Dick, Randy and Nancy. For approximately 30 years in a row, there was a Tryon participating with an athletic team at Glidden high school. Surprisingly, all of the children entered the teaching profession, except Ray. The other 7 brothers all coached in the Iowa ranks. This is believed to be the largest number of brothers to coach in America. At one time, there were 5 brothers coaching football in Iowa. Ironically, these 5 all coached at a high school which was located on highway #30 (the Lincoln Highway). Also, the 2 sisters married coaches.

Dale's current family consists of his wife Janet, daughter Jodie (married to Doug Stokke), and sons Danny, Donnie and David.

Dale is one of those guys that eats and sleeps football. However, he still puts **faith, family,** and **friends** ahead of **football**.

Coach Tryon has coached at all levels: little league, junior high, high school, class 1-A, class 2-A, class 3-A and class 4-A) and college (the Iowa hawkeyes). He has coached during 5 decades. His teams have been crowned conference or district champions in approximately 1/2 of these years. He has won almost every coaching award possible including: **Buena Vista College Graduate Coach of the Year, Omaha World Herald's SW Iowa Coach of Year, NW Iowa Coach of the Year, Coach of the Year at 4 different conferences** (selected by his peers), was the **Des Moines Register's** pick as the **Iowa Football Coach of the Year in 1966, and was selected to the Iowa Football Coaches Association Hall of fame.**

Introduction

It is apparent to me that every coach would like to be better than what they are at the current time. Coaches are constantly searching for ideas and things that will take them to the top of their ranks. I certainly don't claim to be an expert on the subject, but I have coached during 5 decades and I have coached at every level of coaching from little league to college. I have coached almost every sport in existence. Most of my recent coaching has been in the area of football, therefore I have put emphasis on this sport. However, the helpful hints that I pass on to you can be of benefit to any sport that you are coaching. This book will provide true insight into setting up a sports team from the time you take a coaching position until the end of the season and beyond. You will learn a lot about the handling of athletes, assistant coaches, the parents, and the public. I give a lot of helpful hints on proper planning and good organization. Hopefully, these coaching tips will help you to become a good coach and assure you of a winning and successful athletic program. Thanks for taking time to read my book!

Coach Dale Tryon

Dedication

To Janet, whose understanding, loyalty, patience, and support through all of the good times and bad times make her an extraordinary coach's wife and mother. To our children, Jodie, Danny, Donnie and David, who have been and will always be great sources of pride to us. Thank you for all for understanding the pressures of game day.

To my mother and father, Dorothy and Clarence, for teaching me about the good things in life. You taught me about the importance of such things as: hard work, self-discipline, education, sacrifice, fairness, sportsmanship, team work, leadership, decision making, being socially competent, playing by the rules, good organization, having confidence, faith, setting goals, how to win humbly, and how to lose graciously.

To all of the players and coaches that I have had the opportunity to work with. It has been a real pleasure. You have furnished me with memories that I will never forget. You are the reason that I look forward to going to work each day.

Table of Contents

1. Building a Winning Tradition

I've coached in communities where they had a tradition going and I have also coached in a couple of tough situations. Believe me, there is a difference. One year, I took a job as Head Football Coach at Cedar Rapids Kennedy, Cedar Rapids, Iowa. This was a 4-A school (Iowa's largest class). It was a new school and because it was new, no one wanted to go out for football because they knew they would get blown out by the opposition. When they drew the new boundary lines for the new school district, I had several good players in my district. Because they knew we would be horrible, they all moved back to the old district. I had 3 first team all-staters move away. This all happened by the time I got moved to Cedar Rapids. I ended up with "0" letterman that would report to my team. I had to do a real selling job on the new student body just to get some of them to try it. This might have been my best year of coaching. I moved 6 Sophomores up, played mostly Junior Varsity caliber players and we still won three games. At Boone High School, I took over a program that had just recently suffered through the longest losing streak in the state (33 losses). In the last 4 years there, we went to the State Playoffs 3 times and was rated in the top-10 four times.

I think that there are a lot of things that a person can do to get a winning tradition going. Following are some ideas that have been good to me:

1. It's important that you get the community behind you. The parents of the players are always wanting to get involved with the team. Let them paint the dugouts, paint the town windows, help at Awards Night, decorate the stadium, clean up around the field, be a part of the chain gang, film games for you, etc. Then flip it around. Anytime the players can do something for the community, let them do it. Above all, get a Booster Club going.

2. Get a good rapport going with the boys in High School. Talk at their level. If they want to talk about their hunting trip then talk that with them. If they want to talk about cruising main street, then talk that with them. Show an interest in each kid. I probably try harder in this area, than any other, in trying to stay in touch with the athletes in "their" world.

3. Everyone knows the importance of a good Weight Lifting Program. This is an absolute must. If you can't convince the kids the importance of spending time in the weight room, then you should bring someone in who can. I tell my kids that if you don't get bigger, stronger and quicker, then don't look over your shoulder, because someone is gaining on you and he probably plays the same position that you play.

4. Make football fun. When the season is over, the kids will ask themselves if they enjoyed the season. If they didn't, they probably won't be out next year. We

have a fun-type contest at least once a week. It may take up 5 minutes of our valuable time, but it is worth it. For example, we have 3 legged races (using a big sack). The team that wins does not have to run sprints that night or we will award them with something else. We have one business man that brings in "malts" after a hot practice. We have another business man that brings in water melon after a hot practice. The kids like this. It is reason for them to want to come out for football again next fall.

5. Schedule teams that you can defeat. Most teams are restricted to conference or district play, but there are usually a few games at the start of the season where you could play anyone that you wanted. Visit with the Athletic Director about this. Kids like to win.

6. Hire the right officials. There are good officials and there are some not-so-good officials. I have never met an official that I didn't like, but I keep a list of names, just in case I change my mind! There is no doubt about it, there are some officials that throw more flags than others. I recommend that if you are the favorite team you want officials that do not tend to throw the flag and if you are the big underdog, it would probably benefit you if you had a group of officials that called a lot of penalties.

7. Praise the kids constantly. Players thrive on a pat on the back or a word of encouragement. They like to see their names in a paper. If you praise them, they will work harder for you. All of your assistant coaches should join you in praising the players. Also, make hilite tapes and include every player in them.

8. Get the numbers out. I've yet to see a team, with large numbers, have a bad team. Impress upon your athletes the importance of hard work. I tell them, "to work hard and good things have a way of happening."

9. Most communities have a local television channel. They are always looking for things to show. Why not have them show reruns of your last game?

10. Make sure the linemen get the proper credit. It's a good idea to let the linemen be the first on the bus and the first off. Make the backs carry the sideline coats to the game.

11. Let all seniors take turns being captain. By the end of the season, all seniors will have been captain for at least one game. Then we let the team pick their four choices for the last game and into the playoffs.

12. Play a lot of kids. We tell our kids that if they come out for football, then will get to play in a game that week. It may only be a Junior Varsity game, but they will get to play.

13. Tell a joke, each night, during stretching exercises. The kids look forward to these and it takes the boredom away from the exercising.

14. Be liberal with the letters. If a kid is on the border line on whether he will get a letter or not, give it to him.

To me one of the quickest ways to get a winning tradition going is to make sure that you and all of your coaches do everything in their power to be a successful coach. I think in order to be successful, you need to possess the following qualities:

S= Sound Body

U= Understanding

C= Confidence

C= Commitment

E= Effort

S= Solidarity

S= Simplicity

F= Fun

U= Urgency

L= Leadership

Now, let's look at the above categories in more detail:

1. Sound body. The better physical condition that you are in, the better your work habits will be. If you feel tired all day, it is because you have not been exercising, eating the proper foods, drinking the required 8 glasses of water each day, or getting the proper amount of rest. You must set time aside for exercising. Have you ever known a great leader who didn't exercise? No one is busier than the President of the United States, yet they find time to jog, play golf, etc. You are given only one body, you won't be given another one, so you had better take care of it. Treat your body good and it will treat you good. Make sure it gets the proper amount of exercise, the correct food and water, and rest it occasionally. The body says, "if you do the above, it will make you feel better, look better, give you more energy, make you stronger, make you feel better about yourself and maybe even give you a longer life." If you are going to live within this one body all your life, why not make it a comfortable place to live?

Great leaders and successful business men are aware of the importance of good physical well-being and as a coach you should be too.

2. Understanding. In order to be successful in any occupation, you must know your subject matter. You have to understand the material that you are teaching and then you must be capable of getting this information across to your athletes. I recommend that you purchase as many books and video tapes as possible. You should attend as many coaching clinics as your budget will allow. Experts say that if you don't use any part of your body you will lose it. If you don't use your legs they will become so weak that you can't walk on them. The same can be said for the brain. If you don't use the brain, it will also deteriorate. Keep that thinking process going!

3. Confidence. I think every person needs to have confidence in order to make it through life. It is extremely important that each person has some pride in something they have done in life. I have worked with thousands of youngsters in the teaching and coaching profession and the ones that don't make it in life seem to have one thing in common and that is they've never accomplished something to be proud of. They put their lower lip out and become depressed. The ones that do make it have had several accomplishments during their life and they can flex their muscle and brag about it. When my four children were growing up, I tried real hard to make sure that they accomplished something that they could feel proud of: Maybe it was their grades, maybe it was an athletic achievement, maybe it was their looks, maybe it was a musical instrument or a school project. Success breeds success. I have seen this happen over and over where a person has had some success and then they go on to have more success. It is important that a person understands the difference between being "cocky" and "confident." I don't like a cocky person or someone who constantly brags about themselves, but I do appreciate a person that has guarded confidence.

Every time that I accomplished something in life, I felt more confident when I would take on something new. Get rid of the negative thoughts and always be positive and you will accomplish much more in life.

4. Commitment. In any occupation you must set goals and make a real commitment (pledge or promise) to do something. Never be complacent, but always thrive to do your best. Write down the goals and go for it.

Early in my life, I learned the importance of setting goals. I was taught at an early age, by my parents, that if I set some goals, had confidence, and worked hard, I would be surprised what I could accomplish.

In high school, I set a goal of being the best athlete that has ever gone through Glidden High School. I knew this would be hard as there were some great athletes that have gone through this school, including my two older brothers, Ray and Bill. Ray made all conference in football, basketball and baseball. Bill was also all-conference in all three sports and eventually went on to become a Small College All-American football player. Incidentally, I also had 5 brothers come through the ranks after me and they were all good athletes too. My brothers and sisters were always supportive of me. In fact Ray and Bill would hit me ground ball after ground ball and then pitch to me into the dark hours. They were hoping that I would be better than them. Hopefully, I was helpful to my younger brothers and sisters as well. Starting in junior high, I started throwing a tennis ball against the garage door. This was good for my eye-hand coordination. Eventually, I had several of the neighbor boys coming over to do the same thing with me. We did this hour after hour. Our baseball team eventually went on the state tournament 4 straight years. I will always think that this hard work of throwing the tennis balls had something to do with us getting to the state. It got the athletes fired up about baseball and helped them all with their fielding and throwing. I started on the varsity baseball team my freshman year and I led the state in hitting in the state tournament. When I was a senior, I had a batting average of .650 and was offered an opportunity to play for the Baltimore Oriole Professional Baseball Organization. I eventually turned down this offer, because I wanted to go on to college to play football which was my first love. In high school I started 3 years in football and basketball. I was captain, all-conference and all-state for an undefeated football football team. In basketball, I was captain, all-conference , honorable mention all-state, and set school scoring records. In addition, I won the school ping pong tournament for 4 straight years. I'll never know if I was the best all-around athlete to go through Glidden High School, but the important thing was that I learned the importance of setting a goal, having confidence and working hard.

At Buena Vista College, I planned to play football and baseball. Rather that play basketball, I decided to make some money, so I worked in a sporting goods store and refereed high school basketball games in the evening. Our college baseball team won the conference all four years and during my senior year, I was captain of a team that finished fourth in the National Tournament. I was fortunate enough to be a leader in home runs, hits, runs batted in, extra base hits, and stolen bases during my four years of college ball. My biggest disappointment was in football which I thought was my best sport. During my freshman year, I started the first 5 games on both offense and defense. My brother Bill was the quarterback and I was the running back. During the 6th week, I was experiencing a lot of pain in my lower back near the tail bone. I went to a doctor and they decided to operate. After a second operation, they recommended that I give up football. It would have been easy to get discouraged and throw in the towel, but I decided earlier that I wanted to become a coach, so I made it a point to watch the practices and games, so that I could learn all that I could about the game of football. I did this for the next four years. This helped to set me up for my future coaching days. For my athletic achievements at Buena Vista they named me President of the Letterman's Club for 1956-57 school year.

I learned early on that it is easy to get discouraged, but you just have to overlook these downfalls and keep on plugging. In fact, I was turned down in my first coaching interview. I applied for the a job as head football coach at Sanborn High School, which was one of the smallest schools in Iowa. I eventually took a junior high position at Manson, Iowa. They liked my work enough, that they moved me up to head coach after two years.

5. Effort. I've always thought that the harder you work, the better the results will be. In other words, the more you put into something, the more you will get out of it. There are probably a lot of coaches that are smarter than I am, but I don't think that any of them out worked me. To this day, I work on football 365 days of the year. I still view 3 to 4 video tapes every night. I attend 8 to 10 coaching clinics each year. I purchase almost every football book that comes out and I talk football with my athletes every time that I see them. Setting my goals high and working hard has paid off for me many times. Let me mention a few of them to you:

a. Coaching. I've coached during five decades and my teams have won the conference championship approximately one-half of these years. I don't keep track of a won-loss record, but I do know that it will be up there with the best of them. I've had the longest winning streak in the state at two different high schools. I was able to work my way from a junior high coach all the way up to being the Offensive Backfield Coach at the University of Iowa. According to my records, our current team of Boone High School has scored more points that any other 3-A team in the state in the last 4 years. You can see from page 1, that I have received every coaching award possible, in Iowa. My coaching goal is simply to be, the best coach that I can be.

b. Real Estate. During the middle of my coaching career, I dropped out of coaching for a few years. I've always felt that **faith, family, friends and football** should come in that order. I found myself so engrossed in football, that I was neglecting some of the more important things, so I dropped from football for a few years. I didn't know a thing about real estate, but I was determined to be good at it. I started out as a salesman and then I started an office of my own. There were 25 different real estate firms in Ames, Iowa and I wanted to compete with the best of them. After four years, my firm was third in the city for total dollar volume done. I was eventually appointed President of the Ames Board of Realtors.

c. Baseball Cards. During the few years that I was out of coaching, I started a baseball card shop. Again, I set my goals high and worked hard. In one years time, we had the largest card shop in Iowa. At one time I was purchasing 10,000 or more cards a day. I attended card shows almost every week-end. I set up the largest card shows ever held in Iowa. We would always bring in a big star to attract customers. I've gotten a lot of nice autographs and photos this way. I still set up as a dealer at the National Card Show each year. Incidentally, I practiced my card flipping and eventually was the National Card Flipping Championship. They have this tournament in conjunction with the National Card Show each year. When I decided to get back into coaching, my sons Donnie and David took over my card shop.

c. Millionaire. One of the nice things about teaching is that you have a lot of time in the summer to do other things to make money. As I mentioned before, I believe in setting goals high and going for them. One of my many goals is to become a millionaire. I'm not there yet and maybe I'll never make it, but I know my chances would be zero, if I didn't set goals and think positive. Since we have the summers off, I have continued my skills that I learned in buying and selling real estate and I still attend several large baseball card shows to buy and sell cards. In addition to this I have done some photography for a few people, I've over-seen some farm land and have written books and articles.

d. Family. My biggest goal in life is to see to it that my family is brought up the correct way and to see to it that each of them will make it in life. Hopefully, they will put faith first in their lives, have a steady income and have an enjoyable life. I still like those 12 boy scout laws that I learned and I hope that my children live by them and that is to: Be trustworthy, loyal, helpful, friendly, courtesy, kind, obedient, cheerful, thrifty, brave, clean and reverent. My wife, Janet, is a perfect wife for helping me accomplish the above goals. Only time will tell if we have been successful in our family goals!

e. Relatives. Speaking of good effort, setting goals and having confidence, I think it runs in our family. Time after time, I have seen a brother, sister, nephew or a niece make it big in life. Several of them went on to play college athletics. Some made it to Division-I schools and several of them had their education paid for them because of their athletic or academic achievements. There are well over two dozen and still counting. They all had a few things in common: they set goals, they believed that they could accomplish it, and they worked hard to see to it that they did get the job done. One brother, Gaylord, made it to the highest level of education. He is currently the Executive Secretary of the Iowa's Administrators Association. He is the only one in our family to obtain a Doctor's Degree, so I guess it is alright to mention his name without offending the others. Most of the others in the group (including me) have their Masters Degree.

6. Solidarity. You are only as good as the people that you associate yourself with. If you want to have a winning and successful program, you must get yourself some good people to work with. Once you pick out some good assistants you will need to work together. You need a solid basis in order to move forward in your program. You need to have an open-mind. Always let the coaches speak and you better be a good listener. Constantly praise them when they do something good. Mention their name, every chance that you get, in the newspaper, radio, on television, at pep rallies, and on the street. No one should be critical of each other. In this business, you "hang together or you will hang separately." I think that it is also important that you get on the good side of the faculty, cheer-leaders, booster club and towns people. If you have the backing the all these people, you are forming solidarity.

7. Simplicity. No matter what sport you teach you had better use the **KISS** system (**K**eep **I**t **S**imple **S**ister). I have coached every sport, but none is more obvious than football. Football can be a complex system. If coached properly, you will keep the learning to a minimum. Some teams have 60 offensive plays, an elaborate audible system, several defenses and lots of pass coverages. Other teams have 10 offensive plays and a simple defense. My guess is that the teams that have a less sophisticated offense and defense will usually be the winners. Repetition is important and you just can't get much repetition if you have too many plays. **There can be no confusion on the part of the players.** The players must be able to react instinctively. Take a linebacker for example: some coaches will tell him to read the linemen in front of him. If the lineman does this you do that and if he does that you do this. Then they read to the backs and react according to what the offensive back does. They remind the linebackers that they have a certain gap responsibility. I have tried every defense in the world and my linebackers have gotten their best results when I tell them to just react quickly to the ball carrier and to forget about reading anything.

8. Fun. I think that you are going to be more successful if you enjoy what you are doing. I enjoy coaching so much that I can't wait to get to work each day. I know some people that just dread going to work. These are the same people that are unsuccessful in life. Don't be afraid to laugh once in a while. Laughter is a good lubricant for life. It is proven that it takes a lot less muscles to smile than it does to frown. Also, I've always been one to make my practices fun. Each week we will do some kind of "fun type activity." It may cost me 5 or 10 minutes of precious practice time, but it is worth it.

9. Urgency. Don't be one to procrastinate. On my desk I have a sign that says, **"do it now."** I don't mean to hurry through something and miss some important detail. If you are organized, you will **plan your work and then work your plan.** Never put it off until tomorrow if it can be done today. When I set up my daily schedule it works best for me if I do the hard things first. In other words I'll always have a few things that I don't really look forward to doing for the day, so I do them first and get them out of the way. Being organized and getting it done quickly is an important ingredient in being a successful person in life.

10. Leadership. Is there any thing more important than leadership when trying to become successful? Following are some of the important traits involved in good leadership:

a. Good leaders are risk takers.

b. Good leaders are knowledgeable about their subject matter.

c. Good leaders are good organizers.

d. Good leaders have a positive outlook on life.

e. Good leaders are made, not born.

f. Good leaders have an open-mind about everything.

g. Good leaders are good listeners.

h. Good leaders have "visions" and are good predictors.

i. Good leaders are able to surround themselves with good helpers.

j. Good leaders know how to handle failure.

k. Good leaders enjoy life and enjoy their job.

l. Good leaders are loyal.

m. Good leaders are hard workers.

n. Good leaders are disciplined people.

o. Good leaders have dynamic personalities.

p. Good leaders are helpful.

q. Good leaders have a sense of humor.

r. Good leaders are courteous.

s. Good leaders are full of enthusiasm.

t. Good leaders are well groomed.

u. Good leaders have confidence in what they are doing.

v. Good leaders are "take charge" type of people.

w. Good leaders will study how other good leaders do their work.

x. Good leaders have the ability to use good judgment.

y. Good leaders can accept challenges.

z. Good leaders have faith.

2. Being a Part of the Community

No doubt about it. It is extremely important that you be a part of the community. If you take a new coaching position, it is imperative that you move to that location. I haven't always lived in the communities that I have coached in, but if I had it to do over, I would always purchase a home in the community that I coached at. Your school is paying your salary, mostly through taxes collected in this community. Therefore, it only makes sense that you purchase a home in this community and pay property taxes, of which a big share of this money goes back to the school system.

Show a real interest in the community. You'll eventually want the support of the community, so why not support them. Don't ever forget the famous slogan, "Give and you will receive." Following are some ways that you could show some interest:

1. Purchase anything big, such as a car, television, or furniture locally. In fact, it is a good idea to purchase your small things there too, such as groceries and car gas.

2. Diversify your interests and attend several activities around town, such as band concerts, carnivals, special celebrations, local organizations, etc.

3. Anytime that you get an opportunity to speak at a local function, such as the Kiwanis Club, Lions Club, or the Chamber of Commerce, you should do it. In fact, it is a good idea to offer your services, before they ask you. Always speak in a positive manner and talk highly of their community and how much you enjoy your job.

4. Attend school functions other than your own sport. You will want the support of the other programs, so why not support theirs. Don't just go to athletic events, attend class plays, musicals, etc.

5. When you meet new people in the community get a good rapport going with them. Talk about their profession, not yours. Talk about their children, not yours. Find out what their interests are and visit with them about those subjects. Be the first to offer a hand shake.

Assist the other coaches. Volunteer your services. Ask the baseball coach if he would need some help in getting the field ready. Ask the basketball coach if he would need help keeping track of statistics. Go out of your way to be good to them. Do unto others as you would want them to be unto you.

Let the community feel like they are a part of your program. Parents are usually excited to be able to paint the dugout, clean up around the field, etc.

Have many functions where the team and the community are one. A good example of this would be to have a team picnic with the parents. Always introduce the parents and players at the same time. Let the mothers head up the Awards Night. They will love it and will do a great job.

3. The Making of a Preseason Poster

Posters are a good way to promote your program. In fact, I think that they are an absolute necessity. If you do right, you can get these made for nothing.

At the schools that I have been at, I always got a businessman (a real follower of the athletic teams) to sponsor these. At the bottom of the poster, we have the sponsor's name listed and indicate that they are sponsoring these posters.

My posters are 18" by 24." To keep the cost down, we have them made in 2 colors. We use white as the background, with black print and put a lot of trim on it (which is usually the dominant school color, such as red).

Our local printing company charges approximately $1.00 per poster, if ordered in quantity. We usually have between 175 and 200 made up. We see to it that all businesses get a poster as well as the teachers, coaches, cheerleaders and players. Our sponsor always gets a few extras.

I always take our best photo from the last season and put it right in the middle of the poster. Last year, we had a photo where 8 of our players were tackling 1 ball carrier. It was a great photo. Under the photo, we put, **"Don't mess with Boone."** Obviously, we also put emphasis on the schedules. We like to include the schedules of the Varsity, Junior-Varsity, Sophomores and maybe the Freshmen. Following are the things that we like to include in the poster:

1. A favorite photo in the middle.

2. The schedules.

3. Individual photos of all returning Varsity and Junior Varsity members.

4. Action photos from the last season.

5. Photo of the trainers.

6. Photo of the cheer leaders.

7. Photo of the "Gridiron Gals." These are our sideline statisticians.

8. Photo of the coaches.

9. Maybe some silly photos. An example would be to have a player holding twelve footballs in his hand. They are taped together, but it looks real.

10. We always mention the company that is sponsoring these posters.

I turn in all of the photos, etc., into the printers during the late days of May. They will put together a copy of what it will eventually look like. I will then quickly proof read it. They send them away to get made. They are usually back by the middle of the summer.

We usually find a sports fan who loves to be a part of the program. He will deliver these around town. I take the rest and give them to the players, coaches, cheerleaders, and teachers. I always save one to post with the last few years. Players enjoy coming back in a few years and admire their photo still on the wall.

4. The Proper Way to Set Up a Booster Club

Booster clubs are a very important ingredient of a sports team. However, the club has to understand from the start that their main purpose is to support the team. This can be done financially and with general support. I like members that will talk positive with my athletes and pat them on the back when they do something good. In other words, keep my athletes "pumped up" for the next game. In no way should the booster club be a pressure group. If it becomes a pressure group, then you are better without a booster club.

I've been very fortunate to be in communities where they have had top-notch booster clubs. I think I read where our local club gave $40,000 toward the school activities this past year. Obviously, in order to have this kind of money they need to have several promotional activities where they are making some money. The school gives them complete control of concessions at all home athletic events. They sell t-shirts, sweat shirts, caps, shorts, cushions, etc.. They sponsor wrestling contests, grade school basketball contests, etc. They are a very aggressive group. This is probably the best Booster Club that I have ever been associated with.

Make sure you support the Booster Club. You and your team mates should help them out as much as possible. A lot of clubs have the coaches speak on a weekly basis and maybe show hilite tapes of the past game and maybe some comments about the upcoming game. I think this is a great idea. It is a good idea for you and your entire staff to join the club. Encourage others to enjoy the club. Tell your athletes to get their parents to join. Work with the booster club. Have occasions where the team and the club are together. We have a fall picnic for all fall sports teams. We get great crowds. The team is introduced and the booster club trys to increase their membership. The cheer leaders give yells and we play the school fight song. All fall athletes wear their uniforms to this picnic. Each coach talks about the upcoming season.

A lot of good athletic programs have 2 booster clubs. I think this is a great idea. They have contests weekly to see if they can "out do" the other club. Some of the things that have been done to out perform the other club are:

1. Give small footballs to all new born boys in the area.

2. Have a helicopter bring in a coach, mascot, etc., before the game.

3. Fireworks after each score.

4. Canons bursting after each score.

5. Run large flags around the field after each score.

6. Painting of windows or streets.

7. Decorating the stadium.

8. Sky divers.

9. Loud music before, during and after the game.

10. Planes flying over with a banner behind it.

11. Throwing of small footballs into the stands.

5. What to Include in a Playbook

To me the biggest thing with a playbook is deciding what to put into it. The off-season should be spent trying to come up with ideas and ways to improve your book. To decide on these things you need to attend several coaching clinics. They are always full of good tips to improve your program. You need to spend a lot of time going over the tape of last seasons games. Decide what plays worked best for you and throw out the plays that were not effective. However, keep in mind that just because a play didn't go good for you this year, it may be one of your best plays next year. A big reason for this is your personnel. There is no question that your plays should build around the talents of your athletes, especially your quarterback and running back. It won't do much good to emphasize the option play if you only have one quarterback that can run it. If he goes down, you are done. I think that it is good to have some basic plays that you understand and run them each year, but you need to add and subtract some plays according to your personnel.

It is great to have a computer when it comes to making a playbook. If you see or hear of something that would fit into your philosophy, you can quickly change it. Your plays should remain in the computer. If you think that you have heard of a blocking rule that would make this play a better play, then it is easy to change.

When preparing a playbook, it is important to keep it simple, make it attractive, and have given the appearance of good organization. If it is sloppy, the kids will pick up on this and they will not take the book serious. In fact, they will probably become sloppy in their play.

Your playbook should have from 50 to 100 pages. If it is more than this, the players will get bored with it and if it is less than 50 pages, you really haven't put enough material into the book. With this number of pages it would be necessary to have a Table of Contents. Some people like to go directly to a particular phase of the game. It's probably a good idea to have an Appendix, but I have never used one.

My book usually starts out with a letter to my athletes. This is typed on Football Stationary and I usually include some graphics.

Secondly, I have always included a schedule at the front of the book. You should include the schedule of the varsity, junior varsity, sophomores and freshmen, as you will eventually be giving a copy of this book to all players that are going out for football at your school.

You should include information on why it is extremely important that they make commitments to: themselves, the team, the coaches, the school, and the community. If you get a group of guys that have a bad attitude, a negative attitude, or are not willing to make some serious commitments, then you just will not win.

You need to explain why the T.E.A.M. concept is so important. T.E.A.M. to me, means **Together Each Achieves More**. Impress upon them that there is no greater feeling of self-safisfaction in sports (or life) than making a significant contribution to the success of the Team.

Be sure to list any rules and regulations that your team may have. You better make sure that everyone understands your rules on: (1) Eligibility in the classroom, (2) Smoking, drinking, doing drugs, and chewing tobacco, (3) Missing practice, (4) Showing respect for coaches, (5) Use of Profanity, (6) Horse-play, (7) Representing the school properly at home games and on trips, (8) Etc.

When deciding on what to include in your offense and defense for the next season, I think it is important that you spend several hours with a college coaching staff. When I went from a large high school coaching position (Cedar Rapids Kennedy), to being a member of the Iowa Hawkeye Staff, I thought I knew something about football. I soon learned that you would have a lot better offense and defense if you had 8 to 10 minds working together. They are extremely organized. They don't miss a thing. We had several coaches on our staff that went on to coach in the Pros. I think that there were 5 in all. Wayne Fontes is currently the Head Coach for the Detroit Lions. I've kind of lost tract of the others. I always said that if I ever went back to coaching high school football, I would visit a successful campus and see what they were doing. Even though I pattern everything after one college team, I will still always maintain some of my favorite, basic plays that have been with me during 5 decades of coaching. Also, I will always understand that you have to have plays built around your personnel. A lot of coaches teach the exact same offense and defense for 50 years. I can't coach that way. I'm one to try the new stuff that has looked good to me. I've also found that players and coaches like changes too.

The first phase of the game that I usually put in my playbook is the chapter on defense. The successful coaches that I know always put their emphasis on defense. If you don't have a good defense, you'll have a hard time defeating people. By putting it near the front of the book, the players will sense right away, that defense is the name of the game as far as you are concerned. First, explain your defensive theory. Next, include your defensive philosophy. Explain what makes a defense strong. Write about proper tackling techniques. List your defensive goals. Be sure to have written material on the importance of taking away the ball. I think this business of taking away the ball, fumble recoveries, interceptions, etc., is the most over-looked phase of football.

When setting up a defense, start with the huddle and break. Show the gap responsibilities and alignments. Mention what kind of person that you need to have at each position. Show the stunts from each defense. Explain the responsibilities of each position. Show the stunts from each defense. The players will need to see the stunts against all formations, as some stunts you would not want to do against certain

22

formations. You will need to show adjustments for: (1) all formations, (2) long motion and short motion, (3) a team that shifts, such as TE to the opposite side, (4) unbalanced line, and (5) tendencies.

I've been a 5-2 man most of my life, but have changed to the 4-3 the last couple of years. I've probably used every defense known. I don't think it makes a whole lot of difference, but you do need to coach what you know best and according to what your personnel is made up of. I've found it is extremely easy to adjust from the 4-3 to any possible situation and it is also a great defense to stunt from.

Be sure to include your various pass coverages. I know colleges use 10 to 15 different coverages, but I think that 3 or 4 coverages are still sufficient for high school. We use cover-1 (man to man with a free safety) on most our blitz calls. We use cover-2 (2-deep zone) as a change up defense and we use cover-3 (3-deep zone) a good share of the time.

Don't forget to draw up the goal line defense. I've always put a lot of emphasis on this defense. We occasionally use it right out in the middle of the field on short yardage situations. We always go to this inside the 10 yard line. We use the 6-5 goal line defense that has been around about as long as football itself. We make hilite tapes of just our goal line defense. The kids really take a lot of pride in it.

In the offensive segment of the book, it is again a good idea to start out with theory and philosophy behind the offense. Then list the team offensive goals. Next show the proper huddle and break. Certainly make sure they understand that they understand the cadence. Next explain your numbering system. Then draw up all of your formations. I've always been a multiple offensive team, with a lot of emphasis on the Winged-T Trap Series. Each play should be drawn out with the blocking rules for each position. I always list my plays by series, but at least list them in an order that kids can figure them out. If you have a certain type of blocking scheme that you use more than others, you should have a page set aside for that. I've become a real believer in the "zone" blocking that the colleges and pros are using. Therefore, you will find 2 pages on just the zone blocking in my playbook. Emphasis is, of course, put on the fundamentals and techniques (usually with diagrams). Be sure to include a "Hurry-up" offense in your book. Also, be sure to include a goal line or short yardage segment in your book. I've found that we have used this short yardage offense on a lot of nights when the weather is bad (especially rain).

In the kicking game, you would need to include: kickoffs, onside kickoffs, punts, short punts, fake punt run, fake punt pass, punt return (right, left and up the middle), block punt, kickoff returns (right, left and up the middle), and field goals and fake field goals.

I've always felt that the coach is in an ideal position to be a positive influence on the lives of the players. My number one goal in coaching is not to win all of my games, but my main goal is to make sure that each and every person that plays football for me will be a better person for having gone out for football. If I have made a difference in his life, then my coaching career has been a success. During the year, I make a list of things that the players can take through life that I think will be beneficial to them. Many people have asked me for this list. I call it, **"Tryon's Top Thirty-Three Tips To Take Through Time."** I include this in the back of my playbook. For fun, all of the tips start with a "T." Following are just a few of the tips that I include:

1. **TRAGIC** to think that winning is everything. It's the "wanting to win" that is important.

2. **TRADITIONAL** family values should always be a priority in your life.

3. **TEMPTATION** to join the wrong group of people can be disastrous. Never let a bad person bring you down to their level.

4. **THRIVE** to work hard. Work hard and good things have a way of happening.

5. **TRIUMPH** is just a little "umph" added to try.

On the following few pages, I will show you a few pages of our current playbook. I've included information on: (1) Introductory letter to players, (2) huddle, cadence and numbering system, (3) offensive formations, (4) blocking rules, (5) pitch play, (6) stretch play, (7) dive play, (8) counter trap, (9) called pass patterns, (10) waggle pass, offensive practice schedule, (11) the kicking game, (12) onside kick, (13) defensive goals, (14) defensive huddle and responsibilities, (15) a page of stunts, (16) goal line defense, (17) cover-2 and (18) defensive practice schedule.

Boone Football   (Go Toreadors)

My book usually starts out with a letter to my athletes. This is typed on football stationary and I usually include some graphics. Here is a copy of the letter in this years book:

Dear Athlete,

Welcome to another year of football. 1996 should prove to be another very exciting year. Since we graduated 21 of 22 starters from last year, a lot of people have written us off for this year. It is this type of challenge that really excites me.

I've been coaching since 1957 and approximately one-half of my teams have won the Conference or District Championships during these years. It takes good assistant coaches like Jim Paulson, Jim Grider, Bud Smith, Dave Christensen, John Walczyk, Tim Hartwig, Stan Brandmeyer, Dennis Erb, Gary Achenbach and John Bachman. It takes a community and student body that will support you. Above all it takes a lot of talented and dedicated athletes to get the job done. I see no reason why we can't have another outstanding team this fall.

A good part of our success will depend on how serious you take this playbook. A lot of hard work went into putting it together. Take it serious. Know your assignments. The last 4 years we have been rated in the state's top ten. Our offense, during this time has scored more points than any other 3-A team. This year's offense will be just as explosive! Our team has always taken pride in outstanding defense. This years team will continue that tradition. "Work hard and good things have a way of happening." Let's make 1996 a year to remember. God Luck!

Yours truly,

Dale L. Tryon
Head Coach of the Toreadors

Huddle

<pre>
    Y   Z FB TB SE
  RT RG   C LG LT
          QB
</pre>

The center calls the huddle about 7 yards from the line of scrimmage. The front line bends over slightly, with their hands on their knees. The back row stands upright, with their hands behind their backs. The QB is the only one to do any talking. The QB will make the call and will also give the snap count. The signal caller will then holler out "READY BREAK." Every player will holler out the word, "BREAK" together. This command sends the team to their respective positions. Get to your position quickly and go immediately to your proper stance, making sure to get your line splits exactly right.

Cadence

At the line the QB will holler out a fake color and fake number, such as BLUE 19. This means nothing. However, we will have a "hot" color each week for using audibles, then this color and number would mean a change of play. The QB will then say READY-HIKE. There is exactly 1 and 1/2 second delay between the READY and the HIKE. If we have a man in motion he will go on the READY. The ball is snapped on the HIKE. We will quite often go on a delayed count to keep the defense from getting a jump on us. A delayed count would mean that we will snap the ball on the second HIKE. If we are to go on a delayed count, the QB must really emphasize this when making the call in the huddle and also yell louder on the HIKE at the line of scrimmage.

Types of blocks

A. FAN= Drop back passes (FB blocks LB to inside and Lineman fan out)

B. CUP= Drop back passes (FB blocks END and lineman block in tight).

C. TRAP= A lineman pulls and traps on our TRAP plays.

D. COMBO= Linemen join to combo block on I-formation plays.

E. ZONE= Two time block on line and someone will slide off and block the LB.

FORMATIONS;

PRO- LEFT	PRO- RIGHT

```
  Y O O OO O      X     X      O O O O O Y
Z          O                        O          Z
           F                        F
           T                        T
```

WIDE LEFT	WIDE RIGHT

```
Y    O O O O O X           X O O O O O     Y
   Z       O                        O    Z
           F                        F
           T                        T
```

2 TIGHTS LEFT	2 TIGHTS RIGHT

```
  Y O O O O O X           X O O O O O Y
Z          O                        O          Z
           F                        F
           T                        T
```

OPEN LEFT	OPEN RIGHT

```
Y    O O X O O      X     X      O O O O O      Y
   Z       O                        O        Z
           F                        F
           T                        T
```

LOADED LEFT	LOADED RIGHT

```
  Y O O O O O X           X O O O O O Y
           O                        O
   Z   F                        F   Z
       T                            T
```

FORMATIONS;

SPREAD

```
X        O O OO O Y
   F         O          W
             T
```

WING RIGHT

```
X         O O O O O Y
              O          W
             T  F
```

STRONG RIGHT

```
X         O O O O O Y
              O              W
                  F
         T
```

WEAK RIGHT

```
X         O O  O O OY
              O              W
          F
              T
```

TRIPPS RIGHT

```
X O O O O O Y
     O              F W
     T
```

SHOT GUN

```
X      O O O O O            Y
   F                         W
              Q   T
```

ACE

```
     X O O O O O Y
F         O              W
          T
```

NO BACKS

```
X  O O O O O            Y
F      O          T W
```

*The TE and the WB will always align to the direction of the call. If there is no call, such as ACE formation, then the TE and WB will align to the right.

*We can run most of our plays from each of the formations. We will vary the plays and formations from week to week.   *28*

*We may also run an unbalanced line. If we call "BEEF" right, the LT will align to the right side between the RT and Y.

*We will quite often bring in different players for certain formations. One example would be to bring in another receiver for the FB on TRIPPS, SHOT GUN, ACE ,SPREAD AND NO BACKS.

Blocking Rules:

*We will have the following types of blocking schemes that we will need to learn:
1. **Inside zone blocking:** This will be our most used blocking scheme. We will have several inside running plays with this type of blocking in mind.
2. **Outside zone blocking**: This will be our second most used blocking scheme. We will run several plays to the outside using this method.
3. We will have a series where we will have "**trap**" blocks.
4. We will have **drop back pass protection** and **play action pass protection** blocking schemes.

INSIDE ZONE BLOCKING: Linemen are split 18" on these plays. The reason that we like the Zone Concept is because it is simple. We just tell our linemen they have to know two things, basically. They need to know if they are **covered** or **uncovered**. If you are covered and we run an Inside zone play, you do what we call a **Stretch Base**. If you are uncovered you come and help another blocker. We are thinking double team where one of the two will come off late for the LB'er. If you are covered and the backside man is also covered, we know we have a **Stretch Base**, but we are not going to get any help. This is all that we have to know.

If I am covered, the first thing I want to do is to take a Stretch Step. That is a quick lateral step. We do not want to come up field. It all depends where the defender is as to how big the step will be. If the defender is on the blocker, it will be a simple change of weight on the feet. We want to get our belly up field. We want to keep our heels pointed toward the goal line as long as we can. So, the first step is all determined by where the defender is aligned. If he is wider I will take a longer stretch. It will be a quick lateral step. The second step is right in the middle of his cylinder. We step without crossing over. The second step is in the middle. We bring up the hands in the middle of the defenders cylinder and start driving him. If we have help, we are eye balling the LB'er all of the time this is happening. If you do not have help you stay with the defender all the way. It is a stretch step, second step to the middle, do not crossover, rip up. We invite movement and just run them. That is the Covered Principle.

If I am **uncoverd** this is what we do: We tell him to take a 45 degree step and aim for a point on the back of the hip of the defender. If he gets to the man and the hip is still there he stays with it. If the hip disappears he goes up to the LB'er. If he gets to the hip of the lineman he does not come off until he gets to LB'ers depth. So often what happens is they want to come off the block too early. The most important thing is to get movement at the line. Sometimes we drive the lineman into the LB'er. You have to eyeball the LB'er to see what happens. We do not have to worry about who is going to block each man if they slant. We will drill it over and over again and it becomes automatic for our linemen. Just get the defense moving and take them the way they want to go.The thing that hurts the Inside zone play more than anything else is penetration.

29

If the backside guard is uncovered the backside tackle will check out.

Following are some illustrations on how to properly react to a defensive man as he slants one way or the other.

OUTSIDE ZONE BLOCKING: Our splits on the outside zone plays is tighter than on the inside zone plays. We will split one foot on outside zone plays and one and one-half on the inside zone plays.

The outside zone blocking is the same concept as the inside zone play. It is covered and uncovered principle. If you are covered we say you are going to **rip-reach**, and if you have backside help you are going to escape. If you are uncovered you are going to **pull and overtake**. That is all the linemen need to know. We are going to try to get the play outside with this concept. The covered man takes a stretch, and then he crosses over and tries to get belly up field. We want to rip with the hand when we get to the defender to help the other blocker pick him up. We want the uncovered man to pick him up. The man that is pulling just keeps pulling but he must eye the LB'er. If the LB'er plays under he comes off and picks him up. If he doesn't come off the puller will end up going around the man that is rip reaching.

Following are some illustrations to show how the offensive linemen would block a defensive tackle that slants right and left, etc.

Just remember this:
1. For Inside Zone Blocking:
    a. If Covered=Stretch Base!
    b. If Uncovered= Stretch Double!

2. For Outside Zone Blocking:
    a. If Covered=Rip-Reach!
    b. If Uncovered=Pull and Take Over!

Ace, 53 Dive

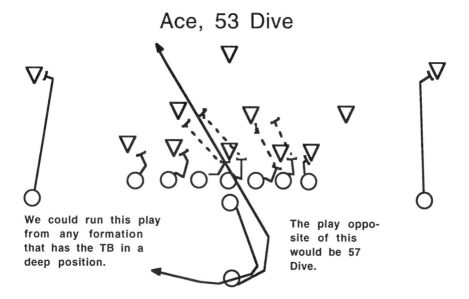

We could run this play from any formation that has the TB in a deep position.

The play opposite of this would be 57 Dive.

All Linemen= Please refer to earlier page on Inside Zone Blocking. One of our linemen will call **Ohio** or **Indiana** at the line on all zone blocking plays. Indiana would indicate Inside zone blocking and **Ohio** would indicate outside zone blocking. In the above case the lineman would call **Indiana**.

QB= Open toward hole and get ball to TB quick at 4 1/2 to 5 yards deep. Then fake a bootleg pass. Do not look back at ball carrier.

FB= If aligned wide, stalk block the cornerback. If aligned in tight, block the defensive end away from the call.

TB= Open. Cross-over and aim for RT (inside leg). If you can get 4 yards in the "B" gap take it, otherwise, think cut-back.

Weak R, 51 Stretch (mo)

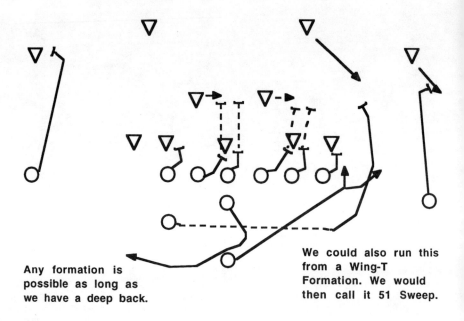

Any formation is
possible as long as
we have a deep back.

We could also run this
from a Wing-T
Formation. We would
then call it 51 Sweep.

X=Cornerback.

All Linemen= Refer to "Outside Zone Blocking" assignments on an earlier page.

QB=Get ball deep to TB and fake a bootleg.
FB=Block the first man outside of "Y's" block OR "RT's" block when going toward
"X". You would be in motion on some plays. Run over the defender.
TB=Aim for one yard outside defensive end. Speed is extremely important. When
you get to end spot (cut up on daylight or beat everyone to the flank).

WB= Stalk the cornerback.

Strong R, 52 Coun. Trap(mo)

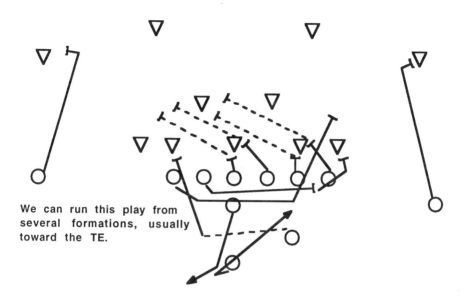

We can run this play from several formations, usually toward the TE.

X=Stalk block the cornerback.

LT=Pull. Get depth on first step. Lead play up the hole.

LG=Pull. Get depth on first step. Log the def. end. Take end out in. If def end comes across the line more than one yard, then you would trap him out.

C=Uncovered (Block first lineman away)

Covered (Combo with SG, block man on to backside LB)

RG=Uncovered (Combo with C, blocking man on center to backside LB.)

Covered (Combo with RT, blocking man on to backside LB).

RT=Uncovered (Combo with RG, blocking man on guard to backside LB).

Covered (Combo with TE, blocking man on to backside LB).

Y=Block first lineman to your inside. Then combo down to the LB.

Z=Stalk block cornerback. We may send you in motion.

QB=Get depth quick and hand off with left hand to TB. Fake a pass.

FB=Block the first lineman outside of the LG. We may send you in motion.

TB=Shuffle to the left. Receive ball. Read block of the pulling guard. You will break this play either to the inside or to the outside of defensive end. Then read block of pulling tackle. Run for daylight.

*Each week, we would run this from a different formation.

Pro Right, 51 Pitch

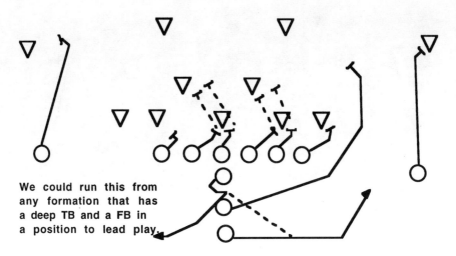

We could run this from
any formation that has
a deep TB and a FB in
a position to lead play.

X and WB= Stalk block the corners.

All Linemen= Refer to "outside zone blocking" assignments on an earlier page.

QB= Reverse pivot. Pitch to TB and fake a bootleg.

TB= Lead step. Receive pitch while on the move. Sprint right and run for daylight.
If Def. end is real wide the TE will block him out and you would have to cut inside
this block.

FB= Depending where you align up, you may have to be in motion. Lead play and
block the first person to show outside the defensive end (usually the force man).

Called Pass Patterns

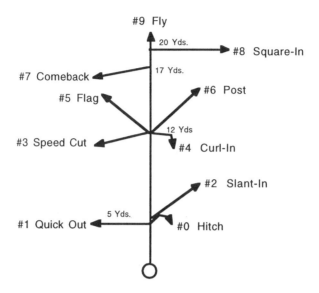

#9 Fly

20 Yds.

#8 Square-In

#7 Comeback

17 Yds.

#5 Flag

#6 Post

#3 Speed Cut

12 Yds

#4 Curl-In

#2 Slant-In

5 Yds.

#1 Quick Out

#0 Hitch

*Our drop back pass plays will consist of calling one of the following patterns;

*X=Split-End
 Y=Tight-End
 Z= Flanker

*Even numbers are always to the inside and odd numbers are to the outside.

*If we are in Wing-Right, an X-5 call, means the Split end ("X") will do a "flag".

* Our "audibles" will also be based on the information above. Our offense will quickly line up in a Wing-Right formation. A Z-7 calls means that the Z back will do a #7 or comback pattern.

*The QB will take the following drop steps; Throw before receiver cuts.
 a. 3 steps= #0,#1,#2 patterns. (1 big step and 2 little steps)
 b. 5 steps= #3,#4,#5,#6 patterns. (3 big steps and 2 little steps)
 c. 7 steps= #7,#8,#9 patterns. (5 big steps and 2 little steps)

Wing Right, Waggle Left

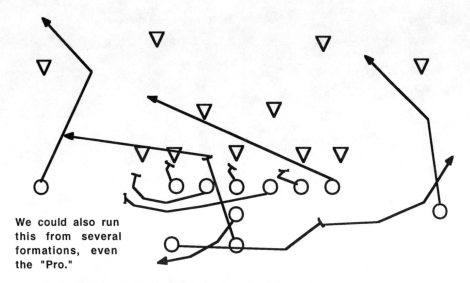

We could also run this from several formations, even the "Pro."

X= Go inside toward the FS and then do a deep flag pattern.

LT= On or first lineman to inside.

LG= Pull, block first lineman outside the LT's block.   Try to hook your man. If QB yells "GO" then lead the QB downfield.

C= On or first lineman away the direction of the call.

RG= Pull, "LOG" the defensive end. Help the LG take him in. If the QB does not get the end hooked, you should proceed to take the end out. If the QB hollers "GO" then you will help lead the QB down field.

RT= Pull, check block for pulling guard.

Y= Cross at a depth of 15 yards.

Z= Run a #6 (post) pattern. Align wide.

QB= Open. Take 2 step straight back. Fake a handoff to TB. Threaten flank (no deeper than 6 yards). Option run or pass. Look for "X", "F","Y","Z","T" in this order!

FB= Block "A" gap. Then go to 5 yards deep in the flat.

TB= Fake a sweep. If backside end is coming hard, stay and block; if not, release to a throwback route.

*This is probably one our most consistent pass plays. It has shown a very high completion rate.

Boone Football=Offense

Period (10 min.)	Coach Tryon (backs)	Coach Paulson (line)	Coach Johnson (ends)	
1	Kickoff returns	Punts	Field Goals	Kicking
2	Progression Drills	Progression Drills	Progression Drills	Individ.
3	Fundamentals	Fundamentals	Fundamentals	Individ.
4	Fundamentals	Fundamentals	Fundamentals	Individ.
5	Group Drills (inside run)	Group Drills (inside run)	Group Drills (stalk blocking)	Group
6	Group Drills (outside run)	Group Drills (outside run)	Group Drills (outside run)	Group
7	Pass Skeleton vs. Def. 7 on 7	Pass Protection vs. Def. 1 on 1	Pass Skeleton vs. Def. 7 on 7	Group
8	Pass Skeleton vs. Def. 7 on7	Pass Protection vs. Def. 7 on 7	Pass Skeleton vs. Def. 7 0n 7	Group
9	Inside run plays	Inside run plays	Inside run plays	Team
10	Outside run plays	Outside run plays	Outside run plays	Team
11	vs. 3rd and big and exotic plays	vs. 3rd and big and exotic plays	vs. 3rd and big and exotic plays	Team
12	Use entire offense against defense	Use entire offense against defense	Use entire offense against defense	Team

Onside Kick

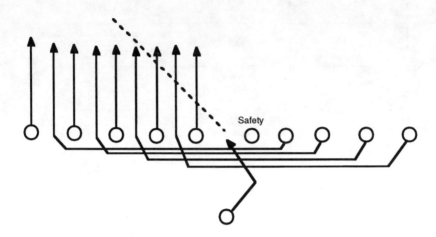

Safety

*All linemen use the same alignment, etc. as they did on the normal kickoff. However, when the kicker yells "SET" the players on the right side of the line will go in motion, as described above. Be sure to get in your right slot. Everyone must fire after the ball with reckless abandon. If you can't get to the ball, then block someone, so that the entire momentum is going the way we want it to go.

*The safety will stay back in case they break a run on us.

*The kicker will align the same as on the normal kickoff. However, before he kicks, he will have to get an angle on the ball. The kick must go at least 10 yards. A perfect kick would be one that rolled about 11 to 13 yards deep and about 5 yards from the sideline.

*We may kick this from the hash mark!

Punt

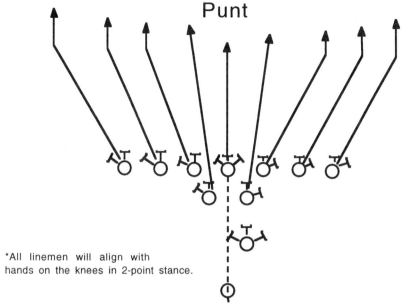

*All linemen will align with
hands on the knees in 2-point stance.

*There will be a 4' split between C and G's, a 2' split between G and T and a 2'
split between T and E. All will step backwards with your outside foot at a 45
degree angle.Keep the inside foot planted. You are all responsible for anyone from
your nose to the nose of the offensive lineman to your OUTSIDE. We are blocking a
zone, so you may have 2 people to block. Extend both arms (outside arm out and
the inside arm straight ahead). Block solid for 2 long seconds and then sprint
down field. Be under control when you make the tackle. All linemen will swing
outward as they are going down field. Everyone turn the play in!. The ends will
aim for a spot about 5 yards from the sideline.

*The Upbacks will align about 2 yards deep and are responsible for any one that
comes in their area (between center and guard).

*The FB will block the first person to show (no matter where he is coming from).
Do NOT step back, as you may block the kick.

*The Punter will be 14 yards deep. Have a balanced stance. Step back with the
kicking foot as the ball is snapped. Take your steps quickly and kick.

*If there are two men between the end and tackle or three men between end and
guard, the tackle will call "HELP-END" and the end blocks inside.

Defense

The Boone High Way

The 4-3 defense is the best possible defense. It is the defense used by practically all of the College Bowl Winners last January. It is similiar to the defense of the Nebraska team which won the NCAA. It is the similliar to the defense of the Dallas Cowboys, which won the Super Bowl Game. Practically every Pro team runs this defense. It is an attack and pursue defense. It involves a lot of blitzing linebackers and stunting linemen. It is a defense that we can easily adjust to any offensive formation. It is the defense of the Boone Toreadors!

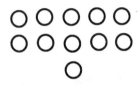

THE HUDDLE
(About 3
yards from
the ball.)

_____

S T M T W

E   E

C SS FS C

GAP RESPONSIBILITY

O   O   O   X   O   O   O
D   C   B   A   A   B   C   D

ALIGNMENTS

O   O   O   X   O   O   O
987   54   32   101   23   45   789

40

Defensive Goals

1. Hold opponents scoreless.

2. Hold opponents to less that 200 yards of total offense.

3. Force 3 fumbles a game and recover 2.

4. Intercept 1 of every 10 passes thrown.

5. Do not allow any touchdown passes.

6. Do not allow any run of over 15 yards

7. Sack the passer 3 or more times a game.

8. Never let the opponent have the ball for more than 7 successive plays.

9. Block or force a bad punt.

10. Hold our opponent to an average of 15 yards or less on kick-off returns.

11. Average 15 yards or more on all our punt returns.

12. Our defensive team must score at least once a game.

"A team with a strong defense will win the close games!"

Stunts from "Base" Defense

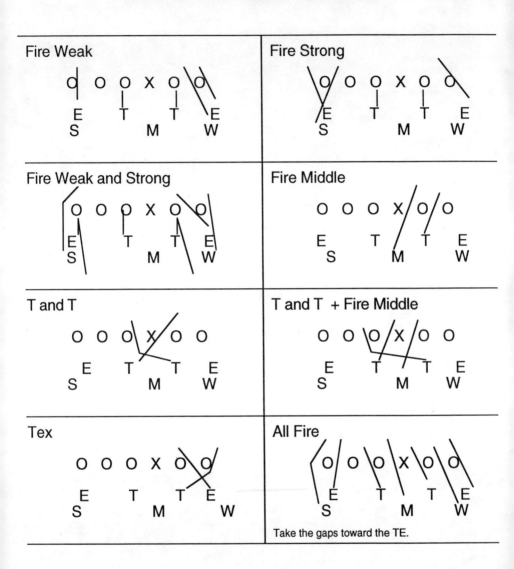

Fire Weak

O O O X O O
E T T E
S M W

Fire Strong

O O O X O O
E T T E
S M W

Fire Weak and Strong

O O O X O O
E T T E
S M W

Fire Middle

O O O X O O
E T T E
S M W

T and T

O O O X O O
E T T E
S M W

T and T + Fire Middle

O O O X O O
E T T E
S M W

Tex

O O O X O O
E T T E
S M W

All Fire

O O O X O O
E T T E
S M W

Take the gaps toward the TE.

Goal Line Defense

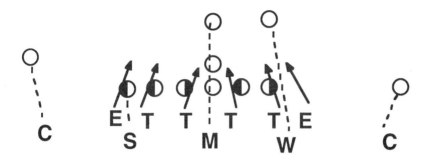

Ends= Bang the offensive end and turn everything in. Take QB on options.

Out Tackles= Align in a #5 alignment. Charge through T's outside shoulder toward the QB. Tackle anything that shows. You have "C" gap responsibility. Stay low.

Inside Tackles= Align in a 2i position and charge hard and low toward the QB. Tackle anything that shows.

MLB= Align in a "O" technique. You have anything inside the offensive tackles. On a pass play, you take the No. 3 receiver.

S and W= Align in a #8 technique about 1 yard off the ball. You have off tackle responsibility. You will take the number 2 receiver from the outside on all pass plays.

C's=Align to the inside of the outside receiver. You have the outside receiver in a man-to-man coverage. Take the pitch on options.

*We will bring in 2 tackles on this defense and take out the 2 safeties.

*We will be in cover-1 with no free safeties!

*This is our defense inside the 10 yard line and short yardage situations.

Cover-2

We will use this zone
pass coverage only as
a change-up defense.

Shown is "Tight" defense.

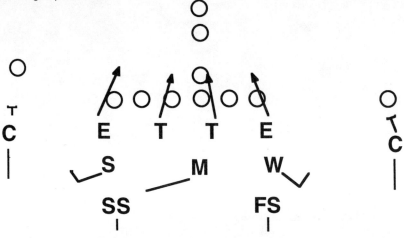

C's= Play bump and run. Stay with your man for about a 10 yard area. Do not go
across field with him. If you notice a 2nd receiver coming to the flat area,
you would release your man and take the flat.

S and W= Drop back 10 yards to one yard outside the TE position. Look for any
delayed pass to the flat, such as a screen pass.

M= Drop back 10 yards toward the TE side. If the TE comes across in front of
you, bang him. Always look for the TE as soon as you recognize a pass.
SS and FS= Align about 12 to 15 yards deep. You have deep one-half pass responsibility. Align close to the hash marks.

*If there is long motion, the SS will go with him and we will revert to cover-3.
S and W must know who has the opposite flat.

*If we call "Fire Strong and Weak" (which means that S and W will be blitzing),
we may have 2 linemen drop and exchange pass responsibilities with the S and W.
Before the linemen drop, they would need to tease the offensive linemen to
thinking that they are charging forward. This sets up the blitz.

Date _____ **Boone Football=Defense**   Time _____
Pads? _____   Practice No. _____

Period (10 min.)	Coach Camenisch (LB)	Coach Klower (LINE)	Coach Christensen (BACKS)	
1	Kickoffs	Punt Returns	Block the Punt	Kic
2	Progression Drills	Progression Drills	Progression Drills	Ind
3	Fundamentals	Fundamentals	Fundamentals	Ind
4	Fundamentals	Fundamentals	Fundamentals	Ind
5	Group Drills vs. inside run	Group Drills vs. inside run	Group Drills vs. inside run	Grc
6	Group Drills vs. outside run	Group Drills vs. outside run	Group Drills vs. outside run	Grc
7	Pass Skeleton vs. Off.	Pass Rush vs. Off.	Pass Skeleton vs. Off.	Grc
8	Pass Skeleton vs. Off.	Pass Rush vs. Off.	Pass Skeleton vs. Off.	Grc
9	vs. Inside run	vs. Inside run	vs. Inside run	Tea
10	vs. Outside run	vs. Outside run	vs. Outside run	Tea
11	vs. 3rd and big and exotic plays	vs. 3rd and big and exotic plays	vs. 3rd and big and exotic plays	Tea

45

6. Ingredients of a Complete Offense

I think that there are 3 very important things involved in setting up an offense: (1) teach what you and the other coaches know best, (2) put in plays according to the talents of your key players, such as quarterback and running back, and (3) keep it simple!

Personally, I like to change things a bit each year. I like to stay up with trends. Therefore, I'm always looking for something new to include in my offense. I like to visit a college campus where they have had a lot of success. College coaching staffs do a very good job of putting in a complete offense. I like to pattern my offense after some college, I've always done this, but I still keep the basic plays that I've run for 5 decades. Also, I always keep personnel in mind. A play that didn't work very good one year might be your best play the next year. I like to run the option series, but if I don't have at least 2 good running quarterbacks, I won't even put the series in my playbook. Some quarterbacks are drop back passers and some aren't.

Every team needs about 7 basic running plays that you would run in every game. Make sure that about 3 or 4 of these are good plays to run on a muddy night, because you are going to have several nights when you will be fighting the weather conditions.

You also need to put into your offense a couple of basic running plays that would be different each week according to what your opponent is going to give you. There is still room for counters in high school ball. I've coached junior high all the way through college ball. Counters are tremendous in junior high, still good in high school but not so effective in college or pros. You need to have a play action pass off your basic running plays. All of your plays should look alike. I'm a multiple formation man myself. Therefore, I change the formations each week, but we keep the same basic plays. I think that we would be a hard team to scout and to form a conclusion about tendencies. Ideally, I think each team should have the passing "tree" which consists of 9 drop back patterns (the odd numbers are patterns going out and the even numbers are the passes going inward). Each team should have several play action passes. We put in one crazy play each week. Maybe a double-reverse, a dipsy-doodle or a flea-flicker. The kids like this type of thing.

In your playbook be sure to include the following:

1. Your philosophy of your offense.

2. Your offensive goals for each game.

3. The huddle.

4. The huddle break.

5. Cadence.

6. Numbering system.

7. Draw up all of your formations.

8. Explain terms for "motion" and "shifting," etc.

9. Explain in detail your different types of blocking, such as "zone" blocking. Use diagrams to show footwork, etc.

10. Explain your different "series," if you number plays in series.

11. Draw up each play. Explain the blocking assignments against all possible defenses. Explain what formations that you will run this play from.

12. You should have a section of "strategy." Explain when you will run each play.

13. Explain your "short yardage" offense.

14. Draw up your "hurry-up" offense.

15. What to do while on sideline. Offensive linemen always be around the offensive coaches.

16. The kickoff return right, left and up the middle must be drawn up.

17. The punt, pooch punt, and all fake punts must be a part of your offensive package.

18. Have a section on field goal kicking, as well as the fake field goal.

19. You should include a section on "audibles." Be specific on this. Know the live color for this particular game. Be familiar with defensive coverages. Know when and when not to call an audible.

One very important aspect of the game of football that I think most coaches neglect is trying to make a good player a great player. Most coaches spend their time trying to make the poor player better, thinking the good player is as good as he will get. This is wrong. I'm constantly giving my athletes handouts (written material) on how to be a better athlete. I also let my players to view a lot of tapes on the proper way to do things. If I have a good running back, I will get tapes of some great professional player and let the athlete study his running form. You'll be surprised how much a player can pick up if they watch film of a great running back. I do this with all the positions, as well as the

47

kickers.

Don't be afraid to copy someone else's great play. Many times I have scouted a team and then we try to defense their favorite plays in practice. If we can't stop a particular play, then this might be good reason to try the play ourselves.

Any time that you get a chance to brag up something about your offense, do it. According to our records, our team has scored more points than any other 3-A team in Iowa during the last 4 years. Don't think that we don't remind the players of this.

Praise the kids when they do something good in practice or a game. It is my opinion the athlete thrives on recognition. They love encouragement. They love a pat on the back. They'll work harder for you. They'll be a better athlete in the future, because you took time to praise them. Every time I see one of my football players in the hall way, I will praise him. I may say, "that was one heck of a tackle that you put on their tailback, late in the third quarter." This kid will be the first to your next practice.

Know the chemical make-up of your team. Some are passing teams, some years you have a running team. Some years you have a blend of both.

7. Ingredients of a Complete Defense

I've used every type of defense known to mankind. Mostly, I've been a 5-2 man, but have switched over to a 4-3 look in the last few years. You can make easy adjustments from the 4-3 and you can really blitz the linebackers. Personally, I don't think it makes much difference what alignment you are in. The main thing is to keep it simple so that there is no confusion in the minds of the defenders. Teach what you know best.

You need to sell your kids on the importance of defense. I tell our kids that as a basic rule, the best athletes will be playing on defense. Remind them that it is defense that wins games. Also, remind them that defense can be a great offense.

It is good to have a few different looks on defense so that the offense can't zero in on you. I think that you need a look where you are headup, on the shoulders, in the gaps and linebackers stacked. I've always like shifting linebackers before the snap and sometimes even the linemen can shift. Work a lot on the goal line defense. Make sure the kids take pride in this defense. We make hilite tapes of just the goal line defense. Have enough confidence in the goal line to use in out in the middle of the field on short yardage situations. Basically, I've been a 6-5 goal line man most of my life.

It is also good to have a few different coverages in the secondary. These coverages should look similar before the ball is snapped, so as not to give away the coverage. I like cover 1 (man to man, with a free safety), when we are blitzing. We use cover-2 (two deep zone) as a change up and we mostly use cover-3 (a normal 3-deep zone). We will use the bump and run occasionally when in cover-1 and cover-2. We always start out looking like we are in cover-2.

A good defensive book will include the following:

1. Your philosophy and theory of your defense.

2. Your defensive goals for each game.

3. Explain what makes a defense strong.

4. The huddle and huddle break.

5. Explain what is meant by "gap" responsibility.

6. Explain the different alignments and the techniques used with each.

7. Draw up each basic defense and be sure to show how you would align this

defense up against any possible formation.

8. With each basic defense, you should define the exact assignment for each defensive position.

9. Show all the stunts that you will be doing from this basic defense. Be sure to explain how you would stunt against each formation that opponents might use against you.

10. Have a large section on the goal line defense.

11. Draw up all of your pass coverages.

12. Know all possible adjustments for such things as: (1) weird formations, (2) short and long motion, (3) unbalanced backfield, (4) tripps formation, (5) a team that shifts from one formation to another, and (6) unusually tight or wide line splits.

Include your defensive segment near the front of the playbook. It will indicate to your players, that you really do put defense first in your mind.

One very important aspect of the game of football that I think most coaches neglect is trying to make a good player a great player. Most coaches spend their time trying to make the poor player better, thinking the good player is as good as he will get. This is wrong. I'm constantly giving my athletes handouts (written material) on how to be a better athlete. I also let my players view a lot of tapes on the proper way to do things. if you have a good running back, find tapes of a professional player and let your man study this tape. He will always pick up some pointers that he might want to try. It definitely will make him a better athlete.

When you make your playbook, include several diagrams, illustrations, photos and charts. Make the book as organized as possible. If the end product is sloppy, then you can just as well plan on your players being sloppy too.

One of the most neglected phases of defense is emphasizing the importance of creating a turn-over. If you want the opposition to fumble, you must have different drills to practice creating fumbles. I recommend doing this every night in practice. It is that important. The same goes for pass interceptions.You won't get interceptions by setting back and talking about them.You must have drills to practice interceptions. It is a good idea to make a hilite tape of all turnovers from the last few years. A great training tool.

Praise the defensive player, when he makes a good play. Kids like to be selected out for a good play. Treat them good and they will treat you good. They love to read their name in the paper and they all like "pats" on the back. They like encouragement. I use to have an assistant coach that would pick up a player and carry him 30 yards after he made an interception or had a fumble recovery. He did this in practices and he did it during a game. He would yell all the way. It is good to have a coach like this on the staff. The excitement and enthusiasm was contagious. Our other coaches and players would pick up on this and get a little more enthused. Tell your defensive coaches to talk defense when they meet a player in the hall way. Praise them on a good play that they may have made or if nothing else, tell them that you enjoy having them out for football and that they are doing a good job.

To me, one of the most important things in setting up a defense is to make the opponent **"do what they don't want to do."** If they are a running team, make them pass. If they are a team that runs the end a lot, take it away from them. Of course, in order to do this properly, you must do a good job of scouting your opponent. Know their tendencies and know their strategies. Along with this, I think it is important to disrupt the opponent. Keep them guessing. Change up your defensive look and do a lot of stunting.

8. How to Make Instructional Tapes

I believe that it is easy to make an athlete a better athlete. One of the methods is through Instructional tapes. It involves a lot of work, but it most certainly will pay dividends. All it takes is 2 VCRs so that you can copy or edit tapes, and a lot of time. The trick is to get your tapes from several sources, such as: (1) tapes from your own games, (2) college and professional tapes that are on television, so long as you don't infringe on copyright laws, (3) tapes that you purchase, (4) tapes of your practices, and (5) tapes of themselves working out. Whenever I see a technique on tapes that looks good, I will mark down the frame number on the VCR as well as what technique I'm watching. For example, I may mark down 154 punt. This means that when I prepare a tape on the proper techniques on how to punt, I will simple pull out all of the ones that I wrote punt beside. In the case above, I would go directly to frame number 154. You might think that I go through a lot of tapes. I probably go through an average of 3 to 4 tapes per night throughout the entire year. I'm sure there are a lot of coaches that are smarter than I am, but I'll bet there aren't many that put as many hours into my profession as I do. One thing that my dad taught me a long time ago was to **"work hard and good things have a way of happening."** I use this slogan a lot. When we take a tough loss, I'll hit my players with this slogan when they show up to practice. Incidentally, the junior high coaches love to use these tapes for instruction.

Following are the different offensive tapes that I make:

1. Running technique, such as: juke em, stiff arm, speed, change of pace, give ground to gain ground, and never running out of bounds.

2. Pass receiving techniques.

3. Proper blocking techniques, such as head on, zone, double-team, pull, pull and trap, drop back pass protection, and play action pass protection.

4. Proper punting techniques.

5. Kicking the field goal properly.

6. Quarterback footwork.

7. Quarterback drop back passes.

8. Quarterback play action passes.

9. Quarterback play in carrying out your fakes.

10.Center snaps to punter and Field Goal Kickers.

11. Obvious penalties that other teams made

Following are the different defensive tapes that I make:

1. Proper tackling techniques.

2. Defensive pursuit.

3. Proper mechanics in punt returning and kickoff returns.

4. Obvious penalties that other teams made.

5. How to take the ball away from your opponent.

6. How to rush the passer.

7. How to stay low on defense.

9. How to Motivate the Coach

Following are some things that I feel motivates the coach to coach:

1. If you want to have a motivated coach, you better be motivated yourself. It is extremely important that you be enthusiastic. If you don't show enthusiasm, then don't expect your assistant coaches to be enthused. Enthusiasm is contagious.

2. Be the first person to the locker room. Be the first to meetings. Be the first to the practice field. This desire will spread on to your assistants.

3. Let the coaches have some say at the staff meetings. Have an open-mind about everything. Listen to them like you are interested in what they are saying. Praise them when they come up with a good idea.

4. Give them some responsibility. Let them have a say when it comes to setting up your offense, defense , kicking game, etc..

5. Let the coaches do their own substituting. They work with the players every day and probably know their strengths and weakness better than you do any way.

6. Don't have long staff meeting on the week-ends. Let them have good family time.

7. Do not schedule junior varsity games on the week-ends.

8. Have a dinner meeting occasionally and include the wives.

9. In the off-season, have occasions where the coaches do things together. Good examples would be to have a golf outing or a fishing trip.

10. In preseason, make sure that you do a good job of explaining exactly what and how you will be doing things in the fall. There can be no confusion in their minds. They should know their exact assignments. They should know exactly how to teach the fundamentals in their respective position.

11. Do everything that you can to do some favorable things for the coaches. I see to it that the coaches get new coaching shirts every year. I try hard to get them free tickets to college football games in the area.

12. Have the assistants attend as many coaching clinics as your school budget

54

will allow.

13. Let them have some say when it comes to ordering new equipment.

14. Get a good rapport going with the coaches. Talk with them in a language that they can understand. For example, if they like to fish, talk fishing with them.

15. Constantly praise the coaches in the newspapers, radio and television.

16. Show a genuine concern for them, their spouse and their children.

17. Make things fun at your practices.

18. Always be positive in the way you treat the coaches. Also, be positive in way you treat the players.

19. Do not have long practices, just for the sake of bragging that you had a long practice.

10. What to Include in Coaches Meetings

I like to start out our first coaches meeting (probably about one week before our first practice) on a positive manner. After introductions, we simply sit around, drink coffee and visit about the summer happenings. Then we get down to some serious business.

We encourage all of our coaches to be there. That includes junior high, freshmen, sophomore, junior varsity and varsity coaches. Volunteer coaches are also welcome to attend.

I usually start the meeting with all of the good news such as:

1. Hand out the new coaching uniforms.

2. Give the coaches information on how they can secure free tickets to the college football games in the area.

3. Tell of any new move-in that we know about.

4. Go over all of the new equipment and uniforms that were purchased since last season.

Thank the coaches for helping out at the summer football camps. Thank them for helping out with the summer weight lifting program. Above all, thank them for talking football with the players in the off season and helping keep them pumped up for the sport of football.

Next, I let the coaches know what is expected of them. Following are some of the things that I would talk about:

1. Make sure the athletes respect you.

2. Make sure that you handle the discipline properly.

3. Never hit a kid.

4. Never put down an athlete in front of the others.

5. Always be positive.

6. Constantly praise the athletes.

7. Never swear and don't let the players swear.

8. Always hustle and make sure your athletes hustle.

9. Expect perfection.

10. Never lose your poise.

11. Take pride in your coaching.

12. Don't demonstrate a block or tackle in a "live" situation with you being the blocker or tackler. You might get sued, if the player gets hurt.

13. Work hard and make sure your athletes work hard.

14. Play a lot of players.

15. Make sure you keep the players interested in the sport of football.

16. Don't let the players quit, it is up to you to make football fun and positive for them.

17. Go over the chain of command - make sure the coaches know which other coaches are working under them. Make sure that they understand that all final decisions fall in your lap.

18. Review physical examinations, insurance waivers and towel fees.

19. Make sure they understand that they cannot dismiss a player from the squad. This must be done by you.

20. Be enthusiastic. Enthusiasm is contagious.

21. Keep trying to make your players a little better.

22. Stay on schedule.

23. Be organized in what ever you are doing.

24. Review scouting duties.

25. Go over who will handle the Junior Varsity games.

26. Help is appreciated in handing out the football equipment.

28. Review the duties before the game, such as who will supervise the locker room, walking the team to the field and warm-up drills.

29. Go over the duties during a game, such as substituting and talking to players on the sideline. Talk of good sportsmanship with the officials.

30. Mention how we will handle the half-time talks. Visit as a coaches group first, then the defensive coach will talk for 3 minutes, the offensive coach for three minutes and the head coach will take the rest of the time.

31. Discuss the duties for after the game, such as handling the press, picking up of equipment, walking the team back to the locker room, locker room supervision and calling in the scores.

Make sure that the coaches of the younger teams concentrate on the following things:

1. The teaching of fundamentals.

2. Make sure the kids have fun.

3. Spend a lot of time praising the kids.

4. Teach them our offense, defense, cadence, and similar fundamentals.

5. Don't let them quit. If they quit on you, the varsity will never see them.

6. Give them some things to cheer about, such as winning games.

Review all of the new football rules for this coming season. Tell them the date of the official rules meeting put on by the High School Athletic Association. All coaches are encouraged to attend.

Make sure that all team coaches have a person lined up to tape their games. Explain how important it is that we get good pictures. Remind them to make sure that the camera man is ready to go, long before the kickoff. Tell the camera man to: (1) start the tape as the players leave the huddle, (2) zoom it in until the TB and all linemen, except the SE show on offense, and include all of the defensive linemen and linebackers , (3) always keep the ball in the middle of the picture, (4) keep taping the play until the play is over and the last tacklers are getting up from the ground, and (5) show the scoreboard after each score. Also, remind them to tape any celebration after the game as this makes for good hilite material.

Go over the entire play book. Use the overhead projector. Have your overlays prepared before the meeting. Start at the beginning of the book and proceed until you are done. This would include such things as:

1. All of the team schedules.

2. Philosophy of defense.

3. Gap responsibilities.

4. The numbered techniques.

5. The huddle and huddle break.

6. Alignment of all basic defenses.

7. All the stunts to go with each defense.

8. Formation recognition.

9. The huddle and huddle break.

10. Pass coverages.

11. Defensive strategies.

12. Goal line defense.

13. Punt return.

14. Blocking the punt and blocking the field goal.

15. Kickoff.

17. Offensive huddle, huddle break and cadence.

18. The numbering system and audibles.

19. Go over each play with discussion on blocking assignments.

20. Goal line offense.

21. Hurry-up offense.

22. Punt coverage.

23. Kickoff returns.

24. Field goals and fake field goal.

It is important to note that when we are talking about specific fundamentals, time should be taken to go thoroughly through these fundamentals. Do the "show and tell" method.

Go over your complete practice schedule. Each coach should be familiar with exact responsibilities. They be should be familiar with our 10 minute segments. We will usually start our with stretching, then to individual, group and finally the team unit. Tell the coaches to practice ones against ones and never to put a large, strong athlete against one of the smaller athletes.

Review what each of the early practices will look like. Make sure the coaches have a clear understanding what they will be doing.

Have a good discussion of the personnel and then the head coach takes the assistants out for a pizza dinner.

All of the future meetings should be give and take sessions with each coach having an open mind as to what each coach is saying. Let's all keep a positive attitude.

11. Setting Up a Football Camp

No doubt about it "camps" are important if you play to have a good football program. You ask athletes to work out on their own, but they just don't do it. This is a good opportunity to practice the skills and get ahead of your competition.

The first thing that you need to do is to get the word out that you are going to have a camp. Send out letters to prospective players and put a notice in the local newspapers. It's always a big decision as to how many grades you want participating. There are advantages to letting the junior high involved, but will you have the coaches, equipment and facilities to handle this many?

Every state is different, but in Iowa we are allowed to have 10 days in which to have locally sponsored camps. They can go to as many off-campus college clinics as they want as long as a local coach is not there coaching them. I prefer a camp of Freshmen through Seniors for about 7 or 8 nights. I don't like 10 days because you can get burned out before football practice officially starts. I would normally have a kicking camp for 2 days, a backs and receiver camp for 3 days and another camp for everyone for 3 days.

You must decide if you are going to charge for this clinic? Again, there are arguments for charging a lot and arguments to not charge at all. I know some charge $20. to $50. per person. In return, the athletes get a cheap t-shirt and the coaches pocket the rest. Personally, I've never charged a thing for my clinics. Maybe, it is because I've lived in poor communities or I just feel guilty about it.

You need to make sure that you have proper staff available. In our state, we cannot let former athletes come back and compete against our current athletes. We can however, let them "volunteer" coach in they have a coaching endorsement. Each year we are lucky enough to have one or two of them. I tell my assistant coaches that we can not pay them to help during the clinic, therefore, they are not required to help out. However, most of the coaches seem to help out voluntarily. The most that I could afford would be to maybe take them out for a pizza dinner after we were finished. It is also good to bring in a former professional athlete in the area, but you have to lookout for what he will charge you.

We insist that each player has a physical examination before they are allowed to participate in the camp. In addition, both the athlete and their parents must sign a paper indicating that they will not hold the coaches or the school responsible for any accident that might happen. Also, we want the parents permission to send their child to a doctor if there was an accident.

The athletes bring their own shorts, t-shirts, etc.. We furnish the equipment of footballs, kicking Ts, nets, goal posts, whistles, a field that is marked off, cold water, instructional tape, etc.

One of the most important things that we do is to tape the kids as they perform. We study these with the kids and then we compare this tape with one that would show a professional doing the same thing. During the year I make several instructional tapes from our practices, our games, tapes that I have purchased, and actual games that have been televised. Kids may take these home to study. You will be surprised to see how much improvement these kids can make if they study how others do it.

Following are some of the things that we would emphasize at a kicking camp and tape:

1. For the punter, it would be: (1) catching the football, (2) proper footwork, (3) holding the hand properly, (4) keeping the arm straight with elbow in, (5) dropping the ball, (6) ball meeting the foot, (7) follow through, (8) hang time and (9) accuracy.

2. For the field goal kicker it would be pretty much the same as above.

3. For the holder, it would be: (1) cadence, (2) receiving the ball and (3) placing the ball on a "T."

4. For the snapper, it would be: (1) hand placement, (2) eye contact, (3) the snap and (4) the follow through.

Following are some of the things that we would emphasize at a backs and receiver camp:

1. Accurate patterns for receivers and how to catch a ball.

2. For Quarterbacks it would be (1) receiving the ball, (2) footwork for drop-back passes, and play action passes, and (3) ball handling and (4) carrying out the fake.

3. For the backs, it would be (1) ball handling drills, (2) foot work, (3) using an offensive weapon such as a stiff arm, speed, juke-em, using the field and change of pace.

Following are some of the things that we would emphasize at an all-player camp:

1. We are going to put in alignments, cadence, and all of our passing game.

2. We will put in a few of our basic running plays.

3. We will put emphasis on fundamentals, even though we can't have contact.

4. Team defensive pursuit.

5. Our different defensive alignments and stunts.

6. All of our pass coverages with emphasis on man to man coverage.

It is important that you have fun at these camps. We always throw in a few contests such as the 3-legged sack race or a 7 on 7 passing camp, with several different teams.

The players are not required to attend these camps. However, we do encourage the athletes to attend the camps and we have had about 95% attendance. I do not hold it against them if they are not there. They do realize that the others will be gaining on them if they are not there. We also recommend that they attend some of the more popular College Camps that are in the area.

12. First Day Meeting with Players

When you meet your players for the first time, after a long summer, you better be well organized. The first impression is the last impression. I always have my first official visit on the first day of practice. You will have all of your athletes in front of you and you may not see some of them again until after the season is over. I'm referring to the younger players, such as the Freshmen and Sophomore teams. This is your opportunity to educate them about everything that they will need to know, to help them have a good year. Following are some of the items that I go over in my first day meetings:

1. Welcome the players.

2. Tell them we are appreciative of the large numbers.

3. Work hard, have a good attitude and you will play in a game each week.

4. We are going to play platoon football so that more boys will get to play.

5. Make sure all kids have their physical examination forms turned in.

6. Make sure they all have their insurance waivers signed by their parents.

7. Have the athletes fill out a form which includes their goals for the year.

8. Explain to them what a good attitude is and how coaches perceive them.

9. Never embarrass another person. Say good things about each other.

10. Praise one another.

11. Be a Team Player. **T**ogether **E**ach **A**chieves **M**ore.

12. Describe what it takes to be a champion.

13. Tell them that football is one of the greatest games in the world. It will furnish more memories than anything else you do in your youth.

14. Go over all of the new football rules for this year.

15. Explain what is meant by good sportsmanship.

16. Tell them never to taunt an opponent before, during or after a game.

17. Work hard and good things will have a way of happening.

18. Always be enthusiastic.

19. Give them a long list of "do nots" such as:

   a. Do not horse around in the locker room or any where else.

   b. Do not wear your shoes inside the school building.

   c. Do not walk on people's yards when going to the practice field.

   d. Do not sit on your helmet during practice.

   e. Do not be late to practice.

   f. Do not abuse any of your equipment.

   g. Do not forget to attend the special occasions, such as team picnic.

   h. Do not pick fights.

   i. Do not complain about anyone's playing time.

   j. Do not make discriminatory remarks.

   k. Do not make negative remarks about someone's physical handicap.

   l. Do not give the trainers a bad time. Appreciate their efforts.

   m. Do not drive your car to the game field or the practice field.

20. Go over, in complete detail, the eligibility rules on passing grades, drinking, doing drugs, chewing tobacco and smoking.

21. Help support the local booster club.

22. Explain what it will take to letter.

23. Tell them that if they want to be a complete football player they will need to make a full commitment to academics, themselves, the student body, the coaches, the local community, teammates, the football program, hard work, and to have a championship attitude.

24. Go over our schedule and explain what it will take to win the district and to

get to state playoffs.

25. Discuss setting their goal high.

26. Be willing to play any position. We will do what's best for the team.

27. Take the stretching exercises seriously.

28. Be able to take criticism. Criticism means we are trying to make you better.

29. You may get a drink of water any time that you want one.

30. Teach them the post practice chant that we will do as a group.

31. Never argue with an official's decision.

32. Do not do theatrics following a score.

33. When being substituted for, always hustle on and off the field.

34. Go over our basic defense.

35. Go over our basic offense.

36. Go over our basic kicking game.

37. Explain how we will check out locks, lockers and equipment.

38. Explain what we will do in our first few practices.

39. Take each position and give the younger players a few things that can make them a better athlete. For example, I will tell the offensive backs :

   a. How to properly carry the ball.

   b. Never run out of bounds.

   c. How to follow the blocks.

   d. It is sometimes okay to give ground to gain ground.

   e. Use 2 arms over the ball when going through the line.

   f. How to use a stiff arm.

g. How to use a change of pace.

h. How to use your speed.

i. If someone is gaining on you, run zig-zagged.

j. Put ball in proper place when in the open field.

k. Don't get excited and fumble after gaining big yardage.

l. How to single juke and how to double juke.

m. Always run out your plays.

n. Carry out your fakes until after the whistle blows.

o. If you want to be a good back, you must be a good blocker.

p. Never run before you catch a pass.

q. Run your pass patterns full speed.

40. Explain, in complete detail the proper methods of tackling, blocking and running. It is very important that we have the helmet (head) in the proper position when tackling, blocking and carrying the ball.

Finish with a positive note and wish the kids luck in having a very memorable year. Then everyone do the new "chant" that they learned earlier.

13. A List of Keys to Success

To me there are two important things involved in measuring success: (1) I think the most important thing in measuring success is whether the athletes are better people for having gone out for football,   and (2) there is the second method which is based on the won-loss record. It seems like the alumni, fans and student body favor the second method. However, for as long as I live, I will believe the first method is the best. If we can be a positive influence on the lives of the youngsters, then we were successful coaches.

I think that there are several important factors involved in having a successful program. Let me give you a list of the ones that come to my mind:

- Get the community behind your football program. Walk around town and introduce yourself. Tell them that you would be glad to help them out in any way that you could. In return, we would like them to support the football program and invite them to come around to watch a practice and to attend the games. Encourage them to join the local booster club. Praise their community as they like to hear this type of thing.

- Get the student body behind you. Compliment them on something that they are proud of. Get to know the kids personally. Show an interest in all activities and volunteer your services as a speaker any time, etc.

- You must be extremely organized in your work. Plan your work and then work your plan. There is one common denominator in all successful coaches and that is they are very organized.

- You must develop some sound philosophies in regard to coaching.

- Know your subject matter. I've never known a good teacher or coach who didn't know his subject matter. Attend clinics. Read books. Talk to others.

- Get a booster club organized. Make sure that is a supporting group.

- Master the basic attack. Every team needs to have a few simple basic plays that they can rely on. You must work a lot on these and run them perfectly.

- Keep giving athletes   sound advice and ideas that they can use as adults.

- Make football fun. When the season is over, the youngster is going to ask himself if he enjoyed the season. Did he have fun. If he had fun, he will be out again next fall. I've always gone out of our way to see that the kids have some fun. We tell a joke each night during stretching exercises. I try to say funny things at practice. Once a week we have a fun type contest, like a 2 man (3-legged race with sacks). The winners get out of sprints that night.

- Make sure that you use the KISS system (**Keep It Simple Sister**).

- Make sure that all players are TEAM players. **T**ogether **E**ach **A**chieves **M**ore.

- Make your players better through coaching, instructional tapes, encouragement, and weight lifting. Athletes are made in the off-season.

- Have the athletes set some realistic goals, both personally and for the team.

- Get quality assistant coaches and give them a lot of responsibility.

- Make sure the athletes have a good outlook on life and a positive attitude.

- As a coach, you should dream of success. When you have good dreams write them down and you are on your way toward your goals.

14. Checklist For Checking Out Equipment

We make the checking out of equipment a big affair. We will have football fight song music in the background. The cheerleaders will be helping with writing down numbers and filling out the checklist form. We will hand out football posters that have been neatly prepared with the kid's photos on them. We usually have some cookies, pop etc..

Make sure that you have adequate help. We usually have a coaches meeting in the morning. I will then take the coaches out for a pizza dinner. If the local pizza man knows that we are coming to his place as a group, he will give us a great deal. The other coaches are appreciative of the fact that I paid for their meal, they will usually volunteer to help me get the equipment ready.

We use a long hall way and put the equipment in neat stacks . The thigh pads will be in one area and the shoulder pads will be in another area. We have a coach in each area making sure the equipment is fitted properly. Our full-time trainer is the one responsible for making sure the helmets fit properly. I personally hand out the game jerseys, because I want to make sure that they get the proper number. If I wasn't there, all of the linemen would probably want backfield numbers.

All kids are reminded that this equipment is expensive and it is their responsibility to take good care of it, keep it picked up, keep it cleaned, and keep it locked up.

Below we show an example of the 5 x 7 card that we fill out for each player.

Boone High School
A football logo

would go here!

Name _____Grade_____ Height _____Weight____
Address_____Phone number_____
Phys. Exam form turned in?_____ Ins. Waiver form turned in?_____
40 yd dash time_____ Bench Press_____ Time in dot drill_____Time in mile____
Fathers name and occupation_____
Mothers name and occupation _____

Equipment checked out:
Locker no. _____ Lock no. _____ Lock Combination_____
Dark game Jersey_____ Game pants_____ Shoulder pads_____
Light game Jersey_____ Equip. bag_____ Hip and Girdle pads_____
Practice Jersey_____ Helmet_____ Thigh pads_____
Practice Pants_____ Helmet Sticker_____ Knee pads_____
Special pads such as elbow, neck, hand and rib pads_____

15. How to Have Organized Practice Schedules

Some of our objectives of participating in our sport are:

1. The participant will acquire and develop special skills in the sport.

2. The athletes will cope with problems and handle situations similar to those encountered under conditions prevailing in the real world.

3. The athlete will develop high ideals of fairness.

4. The athlete will practice self-discipline and emotional maturity in learning to make decisions under pressure.

5. The participant will become socially competent.

6. The student will adhere to a set of rules and will thereby learn respect for the rights of others.

7. The participant will develop an understanding of the value of athletics in a balanced educational process.

The key to having a good practice is to be organized. If you are a coach that doesn't believe in organization, then you better get out of the business. **Plan you work and then work your plan.** My staff always meets on Sunday. We go over the last week's tape and study the next week's tape. We discuss, in complete detail, the strategies and practice organization for the up-coming week. All coaches are given an opportunity to express their opinions on what they think we should do with our offense, our defense, our kicking game, personnel, and drills for the week. We do not leave the meeting until everyone understands their exact assignments for the week. Each week I remind my staff :

1. To accentuate the positive and to eliminate the negative.

2. To act enthusiastic and you will be enthusiastic.

3. To constantly praise the athletes.

4. To make sure the athletes are enjoying what they are doing.

5. To keep in mind that our main goal in coaching is to develop the athletes

into responsible citizens.

6. It isn't what you know, but what you are able to get across to the athlete.

Following are some of my beliefs about a good practice:

1. Never practice longer than 2 hours.

2. Don't run sprints after practice. The running should be done while doing constructive drills.

3. Make football fun.

4. Every minute should really be accounted for.

5. Coaches should coach with intense enthusiasm and discipline, use progressional drills, have lots of repetition, no swearing and simplicity.

6. If a coach goes to practice not organized, it will show up and be obvious to all of the players and coaches.

7. It is worth the money to tape your practices.

8. Always have a full time trainer on hand for all practices.

9. The trainers should constantly check the fit of the players helmets.

10. Never let the players take their helmets off except in extreme heat.

11. The players should be allowed to have water any time that they want it.

12. If a player says he is injured, you had better take it seriously.

13. Move your practices around, so that you always have good grass to practice on.

14. You should always have practice on a striped field for timing purposes.

15. All offensive drills should be done by using our own cadence.

16. All defensive drills should be done by using the opponents cadence.

17. If you act enthusiastic, you will be enthusiastic.

On page 45 you can see our typical 12 (10 minute segments) of a practice schedule.

16. How to Make Good Things Happen

Have you ever heard a coach, who has just lost a game, say, "we didn't get any breaks?" It is my opinion that the team that is most prepared and the team that has worked on obtaining "breaks" will surely get the most breaks. To me the term "breaks" means forcing the opponent to turn the ball over or forcing something good to happen.

In order to have a successful team, you must be a team that has a better turn-over ratio than your opponent. You get these results by practicing the proper drills and repetition and more repetition. My teams have had a 75% advantage on turnovers. This still isn't high enough to suit me, but we are getting better at it.

One of the things that you must do is to change up your defensive look. Don't give them the same look every time. If you set in one defense they will tee-off on you. If you move to a different look, you confuse your opponents blockers. The play becomes scrambled and consequently they may fumble. Someone may bump into the ball carrier when he is not expecting it and force a fumble. I especially like to move around before the snap with my lineman and linebackers. Slanting and doing "X" stunts with the linemen is another good trick to do.

Another thing to do is to blitz a lot of line backers. Don't just blitz to be blitzing. You should have a thorough knowledge of the opponents and know which offensive formations to stunt to. You should know their habits or tendencies. There will be certain downs and distance tendencies that you will want to blitz. Blitzes are to disrupt the opposition. When there is disruption, there are fumbles and mistakes.

Have drills where the defensive linemen are attacking the QB with the hands up. This will give the QB a poor vision when throwing and will help to knock down passes.

I think the biggest mistake made in coaching, is that coaches fail to have drills that practice knocking the ball from the ball carrier. Really put emphasis on this.

If you want interceptions, you have to practice intercepting. Every night in practice, we will practice the pass skeleton for about 15 minutes. We practice the first team against the first team. The defensive coaches must really show enthusiasm when an interception is made. The players will get excited and want to intercept another one. Of course, if you really want to win the battle of turnovers, you must practice with your backs and receivers and teach them how not to fumble. If a receiver cannot get to a pass, we tell them to at least knock it down so that there won't be an interception.

Put a lot of emphasis on the kicking game. When we go 70 yards for a punt return, this was not a break for us. We got it because we worked on it. Our team has been in the top 5 (3-A) schools in Iowa in punt returns the last 4 years.

73

17. List of Proper Stretching Exercises Before Practice

Before any practice, game or even working out, you should always stretch out. This segment should be taken seriously. Failure to properly stretch out can cause a pulled muscle or other injuries. It is recommended that before you begin stretching it is a good idea to get the blood circulating a little. This can be done by taking a jog around the field, etc..

The main purpose of stretching is to gain full range of his joints and muscles. Another purpose of stretching is that it helps decrease the chance of injury.

When stretching never go for pain. You should relax and hold a stretching position for about 10 seconds and we do these twice. We go slightly further the second time around. Do not bounce or jerk. The best way to demonstrate the proper techniques is by taking your best instructor around and have him demonstrate. It's probably a good idea to bring in a professional for demonstration on the first day of stretching. A good coach will always explain to the students the benefits of good stretching techniques.

I always like to start stretching from an upright position. Start with the upper body and work your way down. Stretching is a little bit different for each sport. Following are some good stretching exercises for the sport of football:

1. Ankle grab= Keep your legs straight and together. Bring your head down to your knees.

2. Arm stretch= Put both arms behind the head. Pull the one arm back (grabbing the elbow).

3. Bent knees= Hold the body straight, but slightly bend the knees. Hold this position.

4. Hands up= Put hands far above your head (one on top of the other). Push one hand up with the other hand.

5. Butterflies= Sit down and bring both heels to the crotch area.

6. Hurdle stretch= Bring one heel to crotch and extend the other leg.

7. Back stretch= Split the legs. Lean forward, stretching out lower back.

8. Neck stretch= Lay down with knees up and hands behind Head. Bring up the neck.

9. Long stretch= Lay flat. Arms extended behind head. Stretch out.

10. Shoulder stretch=Get on hands and knees. Hands turned backwards. Lean backward stretching the shoulders.

11. Leg lift= Pair off and lift each other's leg forward, sideways and back.

After stretching out, it is a good idea to stretch the legs further by doing, high knees, striders, cariocca and run and skip. Do these every 20 yards.

18. Some Important Things to Include in Your First Practice

We have had our first big meeting in the auditorium and we went over several important things that they would need to know about the up coming season. Now we have just taken the field for the first practice. I will again have a short meeting. They will be reminded of:

1. Physical examination forms are required before they can practice.

2. Insurance waivers must have been turned in.

3. Talk of what makes a champion.

4. Explain that football is one of the greatest games in the world. It will furnish more long term memories than anything that they do.

5. Tell the kids that they don't have to be the best, but they need to do their best.

6. Review what is meant by good sportsmanship. Explain that they will miss games if they are kicked out for taunting, or any form of bad sportsmanship.

7. Review the eligibility rules.

8. Explain to them that they can have water any time they want it.

9. Tell them that they should weigh in before and after practice.

10. Explain to them what we are looking for in a player, such as attitude, consistency, know your assignments, be tough and aggressive, be in good shape, be coachable, be committed, and perservere.

11. Tell them if they have any problems, they should visit with a coach.

12. Remember, "when the going gets tough, the tough get going."

13. "You're not beaten by being knocked down. You're only beaten if you stay down. "

14. Remind them, that "habit is a cable: we weave a thread of it each day until it becomes too strong to break."

15. "By the mile its a trial--but by the inch its a cinch."

16. "No one on the face of the earth can make you feel inferior without your permission."

17. "Luck is what happens, when preparation meets opportunity."

18. "He can who thinks he can."

19. "A winner never quits, a quitter never wins."

20. Review with the players to work and play hard, listen and concentrate, and perform to their best.

21. Be able to take criticism. If we yell at you, we are trying to make you a better athlete.

Now go over the first practice and explain exactly what they will be doing. Okay guys, let's go have some fun. The stretching instructor takes over.

19. The Proper Method of Evaluating Personnel

The main reasons that we evaluate personnel are to improve the quality of the athlete, to make sure we have the athletes in the proper positions, and to make us a better football team.

Trying to assess the abilities of the personnel is one of the more important aspects of a coach's job. You can judge a player on his looks (height and weight), but you must look deeper than that.

I use the following scale when evaluating personnel. It is based on giving each player points from (1 to 7) for each category:

   a. 7 points for superior

   b. 6 points for great

   c. 5 points for above average

   d. 4 points for average

   e. 3 points for below average

   f. 2 points for poor

   g. 1 point for terrible

The categories are:

   a. attitude

   b. dependability

   c. athletic ability

   d. speed and quickness

   e. toughness

   f. durability

g. strength

h. intelligence

i. coachable

j. experience

k. pride

l. character

I have listed the above in the order in which I feel are the most important. I think the top 3 are all about even in importance. The argument will go on for a long time on which is the most important. If a player has a good attitude, but has no talent, he will not be a great player. If a player has a good attitude and great athletic ability, but you can't depend on him (maybe he will miss a practice every Wednesday), then he will never be great either. He may have the most talent around, but if he doesn't have a good attitude he will be only so good. When I grade the above, only the top 3 categories can receive 7 points because of their importance. Others can receive a high of 6 points.

20. How to Make a Good Player Great

Coaching a good player to be great is probably one of the most neglected things in coaching. Most coaches think that they can make the poor players better, but they spend little time with the good players, thinking they have reached their potential and that they won't get any better. It is my experience that kids never reach their potential, but they can get better and better. It is easy for the so called "stars" to get complacent. Don't let that happen.

I think the best thing that you can do as a coach, to make a player better, is to constantly praise the athlete. Pat them on the back when they do something good. Praise them in front of the rest of the team. One time an old farmer told me that he had a mule and if he scolded it or kicked it, the mule would just get more stubborn. If he would praise the mule and pat it on the back he would get some positive results. I've had several hunting dogs in my day and it is my experience that if I scolded or hit the dog, he would not work for me. He would just sit there and stare at me. If I would pat him on the back and praise him, he would be a great hunting dog. It is the same with humans. We all want to be praised. During the season, I'll meet one of my players in the hall way and say to him that was one heck of a tackle that he made in last Fridays game. This excites him and he will be the first one to your practice that night. When you get on the kids, their lower lips come out and they pout and the poorer they play. Keep praising them and they will just keep getting better and better. If it is a good idea to have one coach praise them, then why not have all the coaches praising the players. This is an absolute must, if you want to be a member of our staff. These words of encouragement should take place, during practices, during games and in the off season.

You have to make sure that the athletes understand the word discipline. Tell them that they will be yelled at and they must be able to take constructive criticism. We tell our kids that we are yelling at them because we are trying to make them better. Be more concerned if no coach hollers at them. Maybe that means that the coach has lost interest in them. Although, I hope my coaches never lose interest in any of our players.

Get a good rapport going with the athletes. Find out what their interests in life are. If they are real girls man then talk girls. If they already know what they are going to be doing for a future occupation, then talk that type of work with them. Talk at their level. If they know you are interested in them, they will become more interested in you. They will want you to succeed. They will work harder so that you can have more success.

At the end of the season and you are counting up the total number of quarters that each athlete played, you should be lenient and if at all possible, give the athlete a letter. There is no question about it, the border line players that receive letters will work harder in the off season to make themselves a better player for next fall than the border line players that did not receive a letter.

Anytime that you get an opportunity to recognize a player in the newspaper, radio or television, be sure to do it. They thrive on recognition and will work harder for you when they get recognized.

Play a lot of kids. I'm a firm believer in two platoon football. If there is one thing that gets an athlete discouraged about sports it's because they don't get enough playing time. If you platoon, a lot more kids get to play. Seldom do they complain if they don't get to play on both offense and defense. However, no matter how large the high school, I believe it is always necessary to play a hand full of kids both ways. I'll always start 11 on offense, 11 different ones on defense and at least 11 different ones on the speciality teams. After the first play, I'll have an all-stater playing both ways.

At the end of the season, prepare a hilite tape and be sure to include all of the players. I try extremely hard to make sure that each player is featured in at least one play on the tape. Most cities have local educational channels that they will be glad to show a replay of the game on their television channel. Kids like seeing these and it will make them want to work harder and to become a better athlete.

Make sure the players have an opportunity for success. There are certain plays that a player can look at, no matter who the player is. For example, if your blitzing, the blitzing linebacker has a great opportunity for a sack and to look good. Let several different players have this opportunity. When we run the quick trap, the fullback usually has a big gain, so we let different backs have the opportunity to look good at running this play. Another way to assure that the players are having success is to schedule teams that you can defeat.

Make sure the players have a positive attitude and a good outlook on life. **"Those that think they can, can." "The will to win, will win!"**

Make football fun for the players and they will work harder for you. Have contests, malt nights, popsicle nights, water melon nights, and tape your practices.

One of the best things that you can do to assure yourself that the athlete is reaching their full potential is to prepare instructional tapes and have the athletes take the tapes home to study. We make our tapes from game films, tapes that we have purchased and games on television. We make the following tapes:

1. How to punt.

2. How to kick a field goal.

3. Proper pass receiving drills.

4. Proper running skills.

5. The proper way to tackle.

6. Good pass protection blocking.

7. One on one blocking techniques.

8. Defensive secondary techniques.

9. Proper fundamentals in linebacker play.

10. Kick returning.

11. Proper quarterback techniques.

21. How to Stay Away From Law Suits

I hope that you all have good liability insurance, because there are getting to be way too many law suits in this coaching business. It can happen any place at any time. It could happen to us in the classroom, on the streets or on the practice field. We can be accused of doing something intentional, strict liability or negligence.

When you start practice, it is important that you point out dangers in the sport that you are coaching. If you are coaching football, you will want to read the labels on the helmet and you will want to point out the proper techniques in tackling, blocking and running the ball, especially as they effect the head area. For your proof and protection, you should always tape any comments that you make to your athletes. Otherwise, some athlete could accuse you of never mentioning anything about the use of the head. Here are some of the things that you might mention at your first meeting about head injuries and how to wear the helmet:

1. Ask the players if they all had their helmet checked by the head trainer.

2. Does your helmet have a label on it and did you read it?

3. Discuss the equipment. If you have great equipment, tell the athletes about it.

4. Explain how you never put the head down when tackling or carrying the ball.

5. Explain the proper techniques in how to tackle, block, and carry the ball.

6. Tell them that we can allow no horseplay. This is when many injuries happen.

7. Have the athletes sign a paper indicating that you did explain the dangers of your sport and the proper things to keep in mind when trying to keep injury free.

Here are some things to keep in mind as you set up your practices:

1. Always have good locker room supervision both before and after the practice.

2. Make sure someone is assigned to be with the kids after the game, both on the field and on the way to the locker room. Keep them supervised until they leave for home.

3. Be aware of any possible problem with the facilities, such as gopher holes.

4. Be aware of any physical ailment that the athlete may have such as asthma.

5. Always have a phone or a doctor at your practices. I always drive my car to practice and I have a portable phone in it. We also have several well qualified trainers on hand.

6. Never let the large athletes go against your small athletes in head to head competition.

7. Schedule competition where the two school are equal in a lot of ways, such as enrollment.

8. Never allow any kind of horseplay.

9. Let the players have a drink of water any time that they want one.

Following are some cases, that I have heard of, where the school and coach was sued:

1. A player injures a neck on the field, it didn't appear real serious at first and the coached proceeded to take the player from the field himself, without using a doctor that was on the sideline. It was later discovered that the player had a broken neck and there would be some lasting injury.

2. A coach shook a player's head and helmet from side to side, showing his disgust. He then struck him in the mouth and a tooth was knocked out. Obviously, there was permanent damage.

3. A coach and school was sued because a player was injured in a game in which the court felt that one team had an unfair advantage over the other school. One of the schools had a very large enrollment and the other school had a very small enrollment.

4. A junior high student broke his neck while attempting to perform a head spring. The plaintiff showed that there was no reasonable progression of instruction in the preliminary gymnastics exercises leading up to the head spring and therefore the instructor was negligent.

5. Two players get in a fight on the sidelines and one is permanently injured. Of course, the courts would rule that they were not properly supervised.

6. A junior high student was injured while playing in a gym class during a game of line soccer. The suit claimed that a physical mismatch was created by the negligent pairing of the students. The court ruled for the plaintiff, saying that the pairing for such a "hazardous" game should have been more

closely supervised.

7. A coach made a very derogatory remark to an athlete in front of the other students. His feelings were badly hurt and claimed that his confidence was lost forever. The coach was sued for harassment.

8. A coach let a player play in practice with a helmet that was too small, because there wasn't a   helmet big enough for him. He participated in a non-contact drill and he got some teeth knocked out. The court ruled for the plaintiff.

This list could go on and on. It is extremely important that because of all of the litigation and contingency fees, coaches should be aware of what they can and cannot do. They need to read as much as possible on this subject. Make sure that your athletes have the best of equipment and facilities. Make sure that they have only qualified coaches working with them. Always have a phone near by and if possible have a doctor close by. If you think that there is a chance of permanent injury, do not move the injured person.

Make sure that you have plenty of insurance coverage. Some possibilities are: (1) an unbrella policy from your local insurance man, (2) your Local, State and National Education Association, and (3) State and National Coaching Associations.

22. A List of Things to Include in Speeches

A coach really doesn't get the opportunity to speak in front of the same group very often during a year. You may get asked to give several talks during the year, but they are usually with different groups. Therefore, if you are going to be speaking only once to a group, you had better do a good job. Your first impression is a lasting impression.

The two most important things in giving a talk are: (1) be yourself and (2) tell them what they want to hear. Each person is a little different type of speaker. If you are someone who does not tell good jokes, then don't tell any. There is nothing more embarrassing, than to tell a joke and no one laughs. If you are talking to the parents of the team, they will want to hear about their children, so that should be the basis of your talk. You must be sort of a politician, in that you will talk on the subject that they will want to hear.

If I were to give a speech to the local Kiwanis Club, I would probably go over the following things:

1. First, acknowledge the person that invited you.

2. Next, I acknowledge the president and members of the local Kiwanis club.

3. Thank everyone for giving you the opportunity to speak.

4. Tell them a little bit about yourself.

5. This is the time that I try to come up with a few jokes.

6. Tell them that the local activities program is one of the best bargains around. Your school offers a well rounded selection of activities, such as music, drama, athletics, speech, debate, student council, etc. You can be proud of your child that takes part in any of these activities. Activities make up only about 1% of the over-all school budget. Yet, it is unbelievable the things that the kids learn in these activities. They are learning so many things that will carry on into later life.

7. My number one goal in coaching football is see to it that my players are a better person for having gone out for football. I want to be a positive influence in their lives. I want to touch their lives. If they come back to me in a few years and thank me for what I did for them or they tell me that I helped train them for life, then coaching has been worth it to me. We all like to win, but that is not the main reason that I coach.

8. Now go into this years team. First, start by telling of the large number of players trying out. I mention that when I took over the job, I had 100 players try out for football (grades 7 through 12) and now we get over 200 out.

9. Next, I mention the strengths and weaknesses of the team.

10. Then I go over the personnel. I try to list 2 or 3 players at each position.

11. Describe your basic offensive and defensive philosophies and maybe mention some trick plays that they may see.

12. Then I go through the schedule, team by team. Mention the teams that we expect to be the tougher teams in the league.

13. Tell them of some of the things that you believe in, such as: (1) that you like to play a lot of kids, (2) we like to have fun at our practices, (3) we believe in the TEAM concept, (4) we believe that, "the fellow who is pulling the oars has little time to rock the boat," (5) "enthusiasm creates enthusiasm," (6) "luck is what happens when preparation meets opportunity," and (7) "life is like a bicycle--- stop pedaling and you fall off."

14. Talk of the benefits of our local weight lifting program. I like to mention: (1) it makes you bigger, faster, and stronger, (2) helps the cardio vascular system, (3) can make you look better, (4) helps the aging process, (5) gives you confidence, (6) helps eliminate injuries and (7) it will make you feel better about yourself.

15. Tell them that the kids enjoy playing football at our school. In fact, we have16 boys who are currently playing college football. I'll name them.

16. Tell the audience that you really enjoy your job. This is a wonderful community and I am blessed with a lot of good kids to work with.

17. Not many people have a job where they really enjoy going to work, but I can honestly say that I look forward to working each day. I feel good in what I've been doing. Coaching has been good to me-I hope I've been good to coaching.

18. Invite them to the games and that they are welcome to come over to watch a practice.

19. Again, thank them for the opportunity to speak to this fine organization.

23. How to Handle Unusual Situations

A person could write a book on the unusual situations that happens to him during his coaching career. Following are some of the more common unusual situations that happened to me and how we solved them:

1. **You have a 60 mile an hour wind to contend with.** I don't ever like to kick off both halves. If my teams are equal as far as offense and defense is concerned, and we win the toss we would probably defer the decision until the second half. Otherwise you may end up kicking off both halves. If the opponents end up winning the coin flip and then elect to defer, I would take the ball unless I had an exceptional defense, then I would force them to go into the wind. When going into a strong wind, it is best not to stop the clock. Therefore, you would not want to throw or run out of bounds. When you have the wind to your back you would do just the opposite.

2. **How do you handle a 0 and 9 season?** I impress upon the parents and the community that we would all have liked to win, but it doesn't always work out that way. Our goal is to make sure that these youngsters have gained from their experience of playing sports. They are better people for having gone out for our sport. They now know how to handle situations similar to those encountered in later life. They now understand such words as; fairness, sportsmanship, teamwork, hard work, self-discipline, character, leadership, emotional maturity, decision making, socially competent, playing by the rules, how to win humbly, how to lose graciously, importance of a healthy body, setting goals, and how to get up after being down. Tell the people that there are a lot of good leaders that will come out of this group.

3. **You are facing a wet and muddy field.** Every team should have a short yardage offense. This is the type of offense that you would use from the 10 yard line on in, any short yardage situation, and on rainy and muddy nights. You must do everything that you can to keep from fumbling. Personally, I like to throw long on a rainy night, because the receiver knows where he is going and the defensive back does not. Therefore, it is easier for the defensive back to slip and fall. When you anticipate a wet night for your Friday game, you should practice with a wet ball on Thursday. Do not run counters, reverses, options and end sweeps, as there is too much chance of a fumble or slipping.

4. **The kids complain about adequate playing time.** Your philosophy should be to play a lot of kids. Put as many different kids on the speciality teams. Play platoon football where a youngster will play mostly offense or defense. It is great for the morale of the team. Play teams that you can get a big lead on and then everyone will get in during the last half. Have a full schedule of Junior

Varsity games. During the middle of the week have a big scrimmage against the second and third team or the kids that didn't get to play much on Friday. Reward the winners. Our kids always look forward to this scrimmage. It is almost as much fun as playing in a regular game.

5. **You have one bad attitude on the team and he disrupts the others.** We've all had this problem. Sit the young lad down and hear his side of the story and let him know your side of the story. If the situation does not get any better, you have no choice but to drop him from the squad. Every time that I've had to drop a player from the squad it hurt at the time, but it always worked out for the best. One rotten apple in the basket will soon rotten them all.

6. **Your linemen can't remember their plays.** A lot of kids don't take their blocking assignments seriously, but as any coach knows, most plays that are bad are because of broken blocking assignments. We do 2 things that help this problem: (1) we give written tests over the assignments and (2) there is always someone on the line that is extremely smart and he can remember the plays of all of the offensive line positions. We have this person say something every time that we leave the huddle. He may say: (1) all linemen are in tight on this play, (2) both guards pull right on this play, (3) there is a double-team block over the noseguard, (4) this play we use inside zone blocking, or (5) listen for the blocking call at the line, etc.

7. **You have a large number of fumbles between the center and the quarterback.** Some years this happens and some it doesn't. It is sometimes real hard to find which player is at fault. Sometimes, I can get one foot away and not tell who is at fault. I discovered last fall that by taping the problem, up real close, you can run the tape back slow motion and figure out what the problem is. Last year, I had an all-state center and I didn't figure he was our problem with all the fumbles, but after I examined the tapes, in slow motion, I determined that he was charging out before he placed the ball in the quarterbacks hands. We had him delay his charge a fraction of a second and it worked out real good.

8. **Your defensive team seems never to make the big play.** You must work on disrupting your opponent and confuse them. The things that have helped me are: (1) use different alignments up front, (2) have the line and line backers shift just before the snap, (3) stunt the linemen, (4) blitz linebackers, and (5) disguise your defensive coverage. Of course, you must practice every day some drills for striping the ball and intercepting passes.

9. **You are having trouble making 2-point conversions.** Some of the things that have worked good for me are: (1) going on a delayed count and now maybe you will have one and one-half yards to go for the score instead of the 3 yards, (2) use an unbalanced line, and (3) option plays are great near the goal line. Most teams don't work against the option from their goal line defense.

10. **You are playing a team that should beat you by 50 points.** Don't try to out finesse them, it won't work. You must go right after them. Take them on right up the middle. If you throw a lot in desperation, you just make the game longer as the clock stops on an incomplete pass. If you go right after them the clock will at least keep running and hold your score down.

11. **Your team has way more penalties than your opponents.** The officials can really control the outcome of any sport, but none is more obvious than football. Several things have helped me to keep the penalties to a minimum: (1) you must go over and over again the proper techniques in tackling and blocking, (2) show them tapes, put out by the local Athletic Association, (3) take the player or players out of the lineup who are causing most of the problems, (4) don't run a lot of end sweeps as this is when penalties are usually called (especially blocking below the waist and holding), (5) don't call a lot of drop back type of passes as this is when holding is usually called, (6) we tell our kick return team that the officials have their hands in their pocket ready to throw the flag as this is the most penalized play for roughing the kicker and clipping and (7) hire officials that are known for calling few penalties.

12. **You just got upset by a weak opponent.** Tell the kids that one game does not make a season. When we lose, we lose together. The coaches had a poor game plan and some of you did not execute very well either. From this point on, we must work hard and good things will have a way of happening. If we win the rest of our games, we stand an excellent chance to play in the State Playoffs.

13. **You have too many backs and not enough linemen.** This is where good coaching comes in. Remember, it is what's up front that counts. Therefore, you better have some good linemen. We impress upon the kids the importance of being a good TEAM player. TEAM to us means, **T**ogether **E**ach **A**chieves **M**ore. Talk to kids individually and let them know that their chances of winning any honors are much greater as a linemen. Tell them that we stand a much better chance of being a great ball if they play in the linemen. You can tell an under classman that we may eventually move them back to the backfield.

14. **You are having several punts blocked.** It's probably a combination of several different things. You must have a center who can snap the ball to the punter with a lot of zip and accuracy. If they lob it, it is almost a sure bet you will have a blocked kick. This is a hard position to fill and the kids should work on this during the off season. The kicker must be quick to get rid of the ball. The linemen have to take this play serious. If you are using the closed formation, each player is responsible for the person to their inside. If you are using the open formation each player is responsible for the anyone from your nose to the outside gap. You must work on the kicking game at least 15 minutes a day or the players will think that it is not a serious thing and will relax during this play.

90

15. **How to defend an unusual formation.** If you are a good coach you will be prepared for anything. We tell our players that if they see anything out of the ordinary to call a time out and we will take care of it from the sideline. Otherwise, the defensive signal caller will just call base defense. The players will align in a base defense and we will be automatically in cover-3.

16. **You have a large number of kids quitting your team.** If this is the case, maybe you should do some sole searching. You have a problem. Confer with the other coaches and some of the team leaders to see if they can give you a reason why this is happening. Most of the time it is because of lack of playing time or they can't get along with others on the team.

24. A Checklist for Things to Take to the Game

Have you ever gone to a game and when you got there discovered that you forgot something? This can be quite embarrassing. We use the following checklist:

1. Eight good footballs all filled with air.

2. Two black field goal Ts.

3. Two orange kickoff Ts.

4. Extra equipment. We take one extra of helmet, shoulder pad, rib pad, pair of thigh pads, pair of knee pads, shoes, game jersey, and game pants.

5. Towels for drying off wet balls.

6. Towels for boys to shower with.

7. Chalk for black board.

8. Coaches game plan sheet.

9. Coaches depth charts for the game.

10. Tape for game.

11. Camcorder and Tripod for game.

12. Opponents tapes that were previously exchanged for scouting purposes.

13. Scouting report on opponents.

14. Roster on opponents.

15. Directions to get to the locker room.

16. Instructions of pregame activities and time allotments.

17. 5 typed out "starting lineups" for the press.

18. A check off list for players getting on the bus.

25. How to Figure Game Strategy

First you must compile a game plan. This includes offense, defense, kicking game, and personnel. It works good for us when we have a coaches meeting and all of the coaches get a say in what our strategies will be. Yes, that includes the offensive coach speaking on a defensive subject.

It is extremely important that you know your teams strengths and weaknesses when setting up your strategies for the upcoming opponent. The things that you decide to do are based on the personnel, strengths and weaknesses of your team as well as the opposition.

When setting up offensive strategies, you will always have some favorite running and passing plays that you will do against any opponent. However, you need to find a another way to move the ball against each team. Following are some things to keep in mind when setting up your offense for the week:

1. Know the injury situation for both your team and your opposition.

2. Do they have a good pass rush?

3. Do they stunt linemen a lot?

4. Do they give you a lot of different looks on defense?

5. Do they blitz a lot of line backers?

6. Do they disguise their secondary coverages?

7. Do they play man to man or zone coverage?

8. Where are they most vulnerable for the run?

9. Who are their slow and quick people?

10. Do they go to a special type of defense in short yardage situations?

11. Do they go to a special type of defense in long yardage situations?

12. What will their adjustments be to our different formations?

13. What will their adjustments be to our long motion?

14. What will their adjustments be to our unbalanced line?

15. Do they use the hash mark location in any way?

16. Do they rush the kicker?

17. Can we try the fake kick (run or pass)?

18. Do they have a great kick return? What type of return do they use?

When setting up your defensive strategies you will have to consider the following:

1. Know who their "go to" guy is.

2. Know the speed of their runners and pass receivers.

3. Who are their short yardage runners?

4. You must be very familiar with their favorite plays. In order to win, you must take away their bread and butter plays.

5. What are favorite long yardage plays?

6. What are their tendencies for all of their formations?

7. Do they use long motion?

8. Do they use an unbalanced line?

9. You must know the injury situation for both you and your opponents.

10. Do they use zone or man to man blocking schemes?

11. Do they trap linemen?

12. When and where do they blitz?

13. What type of passer to they have and can he scramble?

14. Can we block their kicks?

15. Do they try fake kicks?

At the coin toss you will need to consider the following:

1. The weather (wind, rain, sleet, snow, sun, and mud).

2. Do we want to kick or receive?

3. Know your kicking strengths and weaknesses.

4. Know your opponents strengths and weaknesses.

5. Which goal would we prefer to defend first?

The other things that you need to be concerned about when deciding strategies are: (1) the score, (2) the time left to play in the game, (3) the injury situation, (4) the communication between sideline and pressbox, (5) substitution, (6) locker room chalk talks, and (7) field position.

26. What to Include as Pregame Activities

We always bring the kids to the locker room at 5:00 for a 7:30 game. The first thing that we have them do is to show up at the film room. We will look at the tapes of our opponents, even though they have looked at them several times during the week. I don't think that this can be over done. They are told to watch the person that is playing across from them and to find their strengths and weaknesses. They should know if their one great back uses speed, power or shifting ability to make his yards. This is also a good chance to go over any last minute comments that you may have thought of. At 6:00 they get taped and at 6:30, we walk to the field.

Our kids like the music, "we will rock you." Therefore, we play it in the locker room. When we walk to the field (about 3 blocks away), we will follow a pickup that has 2 very large speakers on the back of it. Of course, it is playing the same song. They love to have it on real loud. They think that it motivates them. As long as they think that, I let them do it.

When we get to the field, the specialists will go to the field to do some throwing and kicking with each other. We usually take the field shortly after 6:30 p.m. The linemen go to the locker room by the field. Everyone will take the field for stretching exercises at 6:45. During the stretching exercises, the coaches will go among the group and give them some words of encouragement and maybe some last minute advice. I try to shake the hands of my players. After 10 minutes of stretching, they will break off to their respective coaches. They will work on offense for 6 minutes and then defense for 6 minutes. Of course, if this is a year that we were able to play platoon football, they would work 12 minutes on either offense or defense. We join up on the 5 yard line and run all of our plays against a defense that will resemble our opponent. We usually run 2 teams against a defensive team. At 7:15 the band takes the field and we head to the locker room.

We will be in the locker room for 10 minutes. For 2 minutes, we do nothing. This is the time the kids can go to the bath room, tie their shoes, etc. The defensive coordinator talks for 2 minutes and then the offensive coordinator talks for 2 minutes. Next, I tell the kids that we will shut the lights out and they can use this time for prayer or thinking seriously about the game. The head coach handles the last 4 minutes. I review the lineups, who will be kicking and receiving, the first few plays, other strategies and a few words of encouragement.

At 7:25 we head for the goal posts. It is here that our band forms two lines which stretches from the goal post to the mid field. Our starting line up is introduced and the players will run through the line and then the entire group follows. One week we will introduce our defensive starters and then the next week we will introduce the offensive starters.

27. What to Include in Pep Talks Before the Game

I suppose that I give several pep talks leading up to the game, starting off with our Monday practice. At this time I hit on the following things:

    1. I tell them that I think we have a good chance to defeat the next opponent if we just play our game.

    2. We will need to eliminate some of the silly mistakes that we had last week, such as too many penalties and too many turnovers.

    3. Tell them that the coaches are confident that we have come up with a real good game plan.

    4. Tell them that we match up very well with them.

    5. Tell them that the coaches have found a few weaknesses in our opponent and we plan to take advantage of them.

On Tuesday we mention the following:

    1. This is the day that we hit on good sportsmanship.

    2. Explain what it takes to get a kid thrown out of the game and why we can't afford to let this happen.

    3. Our high school has always had a good reputation for good sportsmanship and we want to keep it that way. The officials will rate the players, coaches and fans and then at the end of the season we will be compared with every other school in Iowa. We would like to be in the top 10% with every group.

    4. Explain what is meant about taunting an opponent, fighting or even threatening to fight, and arguing with officials.

On Wednesday we remind the athletes of the following:

    1. Coaches are told to praise the kids and to tell them that the game plan that we have put in is really starting to take shape.

    2. Coaches should keep everything on a positive note.

On Thursdays we get the kids on an upbeat feeling. They are told that we plan to play a lot of kids. It is this night that any player can get up in front of the squad to say a few woords about the game. Usually, only the seniors will speak.

On Fridays, we head to the locker room at 7:15 and each of the coaches will speak briefly. Coaches are told to not put on a fake front, but to just be themselves. Everyone has their own personality. If your personality is not to holler loud, then there is no need to do it now, as the kids will pick up on this right away. After the defensive and offensive coordinator talks, we shut the lights off for quiet time. The kids are told to pray or think of the upcoming game. I try to get the kids aroused the last few minutes and then we take the field.

28. How to Make Sure you Have an Organized Sideline

Your sideline should be orderly and well organized. There are so many crucial decisions that need to be made in a game, that you cannot afford to have a foul up on the sideline.

I tell my coaches to step in and make sure the sideline is the way we want it to be. We platoon our coaching staff so their assignments are easy. While the offense is on the field, the defense will be huddled in their group, on the sideline, with the defensive coaches. When the defense is on the field, the offense will be huddled with their coaches. As we are standing facing the field, my defense is on my left and my offense is to my right. We try to keep the long benches several feet apart to eliminate confusion. Iowa rules say that we can have only 3 coaches in the box next to the sidelines. When our offense has the ball, my two assistant offensive coaches will be in the box with me. When our defense is on the field, my two assistant defensive coaches will be in the box with me.

We put the trainers in their own area, in between the offense and defense. This way I know where they are always at, in case we need to confer with them. Of course, we have a doctor on our sidelines who roams up and down the field.

We tell our players to be well mannered on the sidelines. There should be no taunting, no fighting, no arguing and to show good sportsmanship at all times. We really impress up them the importance of showing enthusiasm at all times.

Someone on the sidelines, usually an injured player, is responsible for holding on to the kickoff and field goal Ts. I just hate trying to find the location of a field goal Tee, right after we have scored a touchdown.

We also have a full time statistician on the sideline. He gets to walk along with the play. We like to review these statistics at half time and immediately after the game. When the game is over, he will run off several copies of the compiled statistics. This is important information to have as I will usually need this information when the scores are called in.

We have what we call the "gridiron gals." It is their job to walk the sidelines and to help the statistician. They especially help with the tackles and they help me call in the scores after the game.

Don't forget to have ball boys on the sideline. If it is a rainy night, you are going to wish that you had them.

29. What to Include in Your Half Time Talk

Half times don't last very long, so it is real important that you account for every minute. Following is a checklist of things that I go over every half time:

1. The first thing that we do is get the kids comfortable.

2. We check on any possible injury situation.

3. We make sure that they get plenty of water to drink.

4. The first few minutes are their time, where they can go to the bathroom, tie their shoes or to discuss the game with the others.

5. While the players are having their free time (of about 4 minutes), the coaches are meeting outside the locker room to form their next half strategy. All coaches are encouraged to take part in these discussions.

6. When we go into the locker room, the defensive coordinator will be the first to speak. He will have 3 minutes to compliment the kids on the good things, point out the bad things and the changes that we will need to do the next half.

7. Then the offensive coordinator will speak for his 3 minutes. He will also compliment the kids on the good things, point out the bad things and the changes that we will need to do the next half.

8. The kicking coach will talk for 1 minute on changes that we would need to make.

9. I will then review some of the obvious things and changes that I think we will need to make and give them words of encouragement. Remind them the importance of playing good the first drive of the third quarter. This will set the tone for the second half. Remind them that if they work hard, good things will have a way of happening. Go over the starting line ups for next half and give a short pep talk.

30. A Checklist of Post Game Activities

There are a lot of things that need to be done after the game. I keep this handy checklist with me so that I don't forget anything:

1. The game has just finished. You should shake the hands of all the visiting coaches. All coaches should take part in this.

2. While the coaches are shaking hands, the players are also forming their lines to congratulate each other.

3. After a victory, our players get in a group and do their victory chant. To me this is part of the fun that goes with winning. We do not say anything derogatory to upset our opponent. There is no since in rubbing it in.

4. I know that the players don't spend much time in the locker room after the games any more, so I call them together on the field and talk to them briefly about the game and to talk about any up coming events and the next week's practice, as well as next week's game. Also, remind them to stay out of trouble over the week end. Remind them that there is a free pop for them up in the locker room.

5. By now you are bombarded with the press. You must handle these guys with respect. You must be specific and to the point as they are always in a hurry to get their stories turned in. In my case, I have to take care of this in 5 minutes as the radio man always wants to interview me.

6. When talking to the press and sports announcers, always be positive. Try hard to find something good and positive to say. Mention as many names as you can. Be polite.

7. Next, I pick up the video equipment from the camera man. I treat these tapes like gold. They really mean a lot to me and I always look forward to watching them.

8. By now the players have walked back to the locker room. We insist that they walk together and with a couple of coaches. Stay away from the other team as there could be some hard feelings left on the field. If we brought the sideline parkas to the field for a cold or rainy game, the players (under classmen) are asked to carry them back to the locker room.

9. A couple of the coaches will take everything from the bench that was left there, such as the game ball and kicking Ts.

10.Pick up the stats from the statistician and review them.

11. Once we get back to the locker room, we call in the scores.

12. After all the players have left for home, the coaches will go to a favorite restaurant and have a good meal and discuss the game.

31. How to Grade the Tape of a Game

I wonder if every coach takes these game tapes as serious as I do. I probably watch an average of 3 to 4 tapes a night, even during the off season. These are very precious to me. When I go through the varsity tapes in the off season, I turn to the junior varsity games, then the sophomore games, then the freshmen and on down to the junior high. I also copy every college and professional game on television and will watch them over several times. I wonder how many coaches watch the Orange Bowl in the middle of July. I've probably watched the Nebraska vs. Florida game 30 times. I also purchase several instructional tapes, exchange tapes with other coaches and of course, Ive got all of my practices to watch, that we taped. When I get all through these, it is time to start over. It's a good thing that I have more than one television set in my home. My wife loves to watch ice skating. To me, that is like watching grass grow. I've still got a better grip than hers, so I usually win the remote control to my 48" television set.

It is important that you have a top notch camera man, a good camcorder and good tape. Generally, you'll get just what you pay for. I tell our camera man to start the tape as the players leave the huddle and to leave it on until the tacklers are getting up from the pile. The play should be brought in close so that you can see the numbers on the jersey. Zoom it in until you have the offensive team (not the split end) and the defensive line and linebackers in view. It is okay to start out with a wide angle, and bring it in closer as the play develops.

I usually watch the game film right after the game. At this time I mark down the play number and make an asterisk for a play that might make good material for a hilite tape later on. I identify each play by a play number and how many yards we made. We have no meetings with players or coaches on Saturday after a game. I just don't believe in them and I understand the importance of family time. The coaches meet on Sunday afternoon to view these tapes. We study these tapes and also the tapes of the upcoming opponents. All of our strategies are formed at this time, in regard to practices and the next opponent. After the meeting the defensive coordinator and the offensive coordinator will take a copy of the tape and will grade each player that works under them. In grading tapes, we usually use the (+) and (-) method. If they did what they were supposed too, they got a (+) and if they didn't, they received a (-). The players understand this type of grading system. We feel that a player should grade out with at least 80% pluses.

On Monday, we view the tapes with the players. All coaches give comments as the tape is being played. We don't want the players to say anything unless it is extremely important. The coaches will hand out their grading sheets at this time.

At the end of the season we will make a copy of any game for the kids. They may also get a copy of a hilite tape that I prepared. There is no charge for this, as they need only to bring me a blank tape. This is a good way to promote your sport in the off season.

32. What Statistics to Include in Your Post Game Report

We try very hard to keep very accurate statistics. The press is dependent on them and they are certainly beneficial when it comes to trying to get your athlete a scholarship at the end of the season. If you can get the same person to do your statistics each year, you are lucky.

Following are the things things that we keep track of:

1. In our team statistics we keep track of our team as well as our opponents and include:

   a. first downs

   b. rushing attempts

   c. rushing yards

   d. passing yards

   e. total yards

   f. passes thrown and completed

   g. punt attempts

   h. punting yardage

   i. punting average

   j. number of penalties and yards penalized

   k. fumbles and fumbles lost

2. We keep track of team points scored and by quarters.

3. Offensive, we keep track of these individual statistics:

   a. individual scoring

   b. individual rushing attempts, yards gained and average

c. individual passing attempts, completions, and interceptions thrown

d. individual pass receiving including passes caught and yards made

e. individual punting attempts and yards kicking

f. kickoff returns

4. Defensively, we keep track of the following:

a. individual tackles

b. individual sacks to quarterback

c. individual losses to running backs

d. forced fumbles

e. fumble recoveries

f. passes knocked down

g. passes intercepted

h. punt returns

i. blocked kicks

j. kickoff attempts and yards kicked

At the end of the season, we compile all of the statistics and put them into a nice booklet. We also include in this book such things as: newspaper clippings, honors won, team roster, and individual photos of each player.

33. Close the Folder on the Last Opponent

By closing the folder on the last opponent, I mean that we will put a lot of information into the folder of the last team played and it will be there waiting for us when the next fall comes around. If you don't write these things down right after playing them and file them away, there is too good of a chance that you will forget something. It could be the difference between winning and losing.

The following is a checklist of things that I want to put into the folder:

1. Jot down the offensive plays that worked best for you.

2. Write down the offensive plays that were the worst plays for you.

3. If I had to do it over again, what offensive plays do I wish that I would have had in our offensive game plan.

4. Include a team roster.

5. Jot notes about their cadence.

6. Include the defensive looks and stunts that worked best for us.

7. Write down the defensive stunts that worked best for us.

8. Write down the defensive looks and stunts that backfired for us.

9. If I had to do it over again, what defensive things would I wish that I would have had in our defensive game plan.

10. How many starters do they have returning?

11. Include comments that you may have heard from other coaches.

12. How did they handle our double tight end set up?

13. How did they adjust to our long motion?

14. How did they adjust to our unbalanced line?

15. Were we able to get them to jump on our delayed count?

16. Include all the statistics from the game.

17. Include things that you witnessed as you saw them play in other games, either in playoff games or elsewhere.

18. Information that I gained from watching their under classmen play.

19. Other coaches comments as to what we should and should not have used against them.

20. What are their bread and butter plays that we must stop?

21. Do you expect them to make any basic changes next year in their offense, defense or kicking strategies?

34. The Necessary Things Involved in Scouting an Opponent

Scouting an opponent is an absolute must if you hope to have a reasonable chance to defeat your opponent. You can either scout the opposition in person or exchange tapes with the other coach . You can do both if you want to. In our state, we exchange 2 tapes with the opponent. Each District does a little bit different. In our District we send

our 2 tapes after each game. They go to our next 2 opponents. Therefore, if you are on the receiving end, you can expect to get a tape on Tuesday (the week before the game) and a tape on Tuesday (during the week of the game). This method works real good.

If you platoon the coaching staff, you should break down the tapes to offense and defense.

The offensive coaches will want to look at the following things:

1. Where are their basic strengths located?

2. Where are their basic weaknesses located?

3. What alignments and techniques do the defensive linemen use?

4. Do the linemen slant, gap charge, head-up, crossing stunts, etc.?

5. How would they line up against all of our different formations?

6. Do they show any tendencies on their slants and other stunts?

7. How effective of a pass rush do they have?

8. Do they have any hash mark tendencies?

9. Are they more of a "read" or "attack" type defense?

10. What type of coverage do they use?

11. Are they basically a zone or man-to-man team?

12. Do they do a good job of camouflaging their coverage?

13. How will they adjust to our unbalanced line?

14. How often do they blitz linebackers?

15. Do they blitz to the strong or weak side the most?

16. Do they have any particular tendencies of when they will blitz?

17. Do they have any particular tendencies on where they will blitz?

18. Do they consider the hash marks when they blitz?

19. Who are their best blitzers and pass rushers?

20. Did they have any defensive players injured this game?

21. How will they adjust to our long motion?

22. How will they adjust to two tight ends?

23. Know their punt coverage.

24. Look for ways we can run some fake kicks.

25. How to they try to block kicks?

Our defensive coaches will examine their tape and look for the following things:

1. What are their basic strengths?

2. What are their basic weaknesses?

3. We need to know all of the formations that they use.

4. We will need to draw up all plays that they run from each formation.

5. Do they have a basic formation?

6. Do they use a particular formation on short yardage situations?

7. Do they use a particular formation on long yardage situations?

8. Know their favorite running plays and when they run them.

9. Know their favorite passing plays and when they will use them.

10. Be familiar with any tendencies that they might have.

11. Who are their best runners and what are their best qualities?

12. Who are their best receivers and what are their best qualities?

13. Know the speed of the their speciality players.

14. Know the blocking schemes used by the offensive linemen.

15. Picture in your mind what defensive scheme will work best for us.

16. What type of pass protection do they use?

17. Does QB use the 3, 5 or 7 step drop? Do they use play action+boot passes?

18. Do they have any exotic type plays and what are their counter plays?

19. Does the QB run bootleg type plays?

20. Is the QB a capable runner or scrambler?

21. How often do they run each play?

22. Do they run an unbalanced line?

23. Do they use two tight ends?

24. Do they use long motion?

25. Do they use Tripps or any other weird formation?

26. Do they use the open or closed punt formation? Is he a good punter?

27. Did they try any fake kicks (running or passing)?

28. Did they have any offensive player injured?

30. Know the cadence used by the opposition.

31. Know where the TE aligns in the huddle, as we align our defense to him.

31. Do they do a good job of picking up blitzing line backers?

32. Can the QB handle pressure?

When we set up our blitzing package, some of the things that we consider are: (1) To stop the pass we will blitz from the middle on their 3-step drops, if they use 7-step drop passes, we will use a lot of blitzes from the outside and inside. (2) If they are a Two tight end team, we will blitz from the outside. (3) If a teams runs a lot to their tight end side, we will blitz a lot to that side. Of course, the reason that we blitz is to disrupt a dominant running team to confuse their offensive linemen and to rush the passer.

We try hard to get our opponents in a 2nd and 8 or worse situation at least 80% of the time. On third down we hope to be successful at least 80% of the time.

When we blitz we are either in a man-to-man (with a free safety) or we will rush the 2 outside linebackers and 2 linemen. When we do this we will drop off two defensive linemen and play a zone defense.

35. Things to Include on the Bulletin Board Between Games

Here is an opportunity to help motivate the athletes and to show them that you are an organized person and are doing everything in your power to have a winning and successful program.

I think that the bulletin board between games should consist of the following things:

1. Complete statistics from last week's game.

2. An accumulative set of statistics which include all games.

3. Complete conference or district statistics up to this point.

4. Use 3 or 4 motivational slogans for the upcoming week. Change these each week.

5. Keep team statistics and have charts to see if you are reaching your defensive and offensive goals for the season. Keep them up dated each week.

6. For your program in general, I think it is a good idea to always have on the bulletin board: (1) names of those who are currently playing college football from your school, (2) a list of those from your school, that have played at least a year of college football, (3) a permanent record board which keeps track of longest run, most tackles in a game, etc., (4) brag up your past records or state playoffs record, and (5) things that are positive about football in general.

7. Have a special slogan of the week for the up-coming opponent.

8. Have a board which has information about the up-coming opponent. Include information on: (1) their strengths, (2) their favorite plays, (3) their favorite defensive look, (4) their past accomplishments, (5) their roster, (6) their starting line up, and (7) newspaper clippings about their team.

9. Include your practice schedule for the night.

10. Mention the upcoming games of the under classmen.

11. If you are having a good year, include the conference rankings and the state's ratings. If you kids are good, let them know it. They play better when they think that they are good.

36. Things to Include in Preparing for the Playoffs

Well, you have made the playoffs, everyone has celebrated and now it is time to make sure that you are well prepared for the playoffs. Get all of that paper work done first and believe me there is a lot to do. It must be done honestly and accurately or you could even be forced to forfeit the game. The State Association is the one that you need to be exact on. They will want the names of all the people that will be involved with the team. You will need to have a complete roster of the players, the names of the cheerleaders, your assistant coaches, statistician, trainers, press box people, etc.. You will be told the maximum number of each group that you will be allowed to have. In no way can you go over these numbers. If you are told that you can have 55 varsity players on the roster and you don't have that many, I would recommend that you bring up a few sophomores. This will really get these guys pumped up for their future years in football.

Next, make sure that you have the student body and the community really into this game. Make it appear as if it is a once in a life time event. The pep rallies should be special. I recommend that the rally be in a different place than normal (maybe the local park or outside the school house). Get special speakers for this special occasion. The community could paint windows and streets as well as place signs around town. Maybe, put a good luck sign in the yard of each player and coach.

Get a special chartered bus for the occasion. Get one that will have a TV and VCR in it. You could watch some motivational tapes or movies on the way to the game.

Plan on spending a lot of time with the press and television. You will be surprised on how many people will contact you about interviews, line-ups, quotes, etc.

Now it is time to get the team ready. It is always nice to have some fun at practice, but I think these few days, leading up to the playoffs, better be very serious times. The coaches will need to spend countless hours going over the opponents tapes. Most states allow a tape exchange of 2 to 3 tapes. Give them some special handouts so that they can take them home to review. Give them a test over opponents tendencies, etc..

Following are some other things that you will need to do for the game:

1. Make sure you know which teams wear dark jersey and practice accordingly and will they furnish towels.

2. Know where and when to report to the stadium, where you will enter the field for warm ups, pregame practice times, etc.

37. A Complete Checklist For Checking in Equipment at End of Season

There are 2 different times that equipment could be checked in. They both have their advantages and disadvantages:

1. The best time might be right after the game. The advantages are that will you will basically have everything done and won't have to mess with it later on. The disadvantages are that you have a hard time getting enough help, someone will have to wash the clothing as it will all come back dirty and the players are always in a big toot to get away from the locker room after a game. If the last game was an away game, it will be an even bigger problem.

2. The other option is to have the players take all the equipment home with them, hopefully in a travel bag. They can wash everything and bring the bag back to school as soon as possible. The obvious advantage of this method is that the equipment will usually come in pretty well cleaned up. Another advantage would be that I can go home right after the last game. I would take these bags and check in the equipment one at a time in my leisure. The obvious big disadvantage is that the equipment does not all get back in right away. You'll be reminding some of the players, right up to Christmas time, trying to get it all back to you.

Following is a copy of the 5X7 card that we fill in at the start of the season. We will use this same card to check things in at the end of the season. The players are responsible for turning in all equipment. If they are short something, they will pay for it.

Boone High School   A football logo
                         would go here!

Name _____Grade_____ Height _____Weight____
Address_____Phone number_____
Phys. Exam form turned in?_____ Ins. Waiver form turned in?_____
40 yd dash time_____ Bench Press_____ Time in dot drill_____Time in mile____
Fathers name and occupation_____
Mothers name and occupation _____

Equipment checked out:

Locker no. _____ Lock no. _____ Lock Combination_____
Dark game Jersey_____ Game pants_____ Shoulder pads_____
Light game Jersey_____ Equip. bag_____ Hip and Girdle pads_____
Practice Jersey_____ Helmet_____ Thigh pads_____
Practice Pants_____ Helmet Sticker_____ Knee pads_____
Special pads such as elbow, neck, hand and rib pads_____

38. How to Make a Season Ending Hilite Tape

In order to make a good hilite tape, you must have good tapes to copy. A good start is make sure that you have a good camcorder. The best, of course, is the Super VHS. This is a camera that costs in the neighborhood of $3,000. It is by far superior to the normal VHS camcorder that most of us use. I've never been fortunate enough to have the Super VHS, but a lot of my opponents have them. I've seen the finished product and they are much superior. However, if you have a Super VHS, you must also purchase a VCR that will play this type of tape. You should have a zoom lens on your camera of at least 12 to 1. Ours is 24 to 1 and I like it a lot. Next, there is definitely a difference in the quality of the tapes that you purchase. Experiment a lot in the early season (taping practices) etc., and then settle on one that fits you personally.

At a practice when we have our game uniforms on, I have each player stand in front of the camcorder and give his name, grade, and position. This will be a part of the hilite tape to be made later on. Also, take pictures of the entire squad on picture day.

During the season we will tape a lot of different things as you never know what will look good for your final tape. We tape practices, stretching exercises, pep rallies, team picnics, team celebrations, awards night, getting on a chartered bus as we take off to the State Playoffs, window paintings, fireworks, bonfires, yards signs, etc..

Train your camera man to get to the game early, so that he doesn't miss a thing. Also, there is sometimes a race to get the best location in or on the press box. Do not take a picture through a window. It will be a blurry picture. Start the picture, just when the team breaks from the huddle. The size of the picture should include the Tailback on offense (as well as end to end), but not necessarily the split end. The defense will include the line and linebackers. If you try to include all defensive backs, the picture will be so far away that you won't be able to read the numbers of the players. A good camera man might take a picture from a distance and then bring it in closer before the ball is snapped. Try to always keep the ball in the center if the picture. After the ball carrier is tackled, the camera man should leave the camera going for a few more seconds. I like to see who made the tackles and sometimes you can't tell until the players are getting up. Do not run the camera between plays or you will have yourself a tape that will be way to long. Tell your camera man to tape any celebration after the game. This makes good hilite material later on. Of course, show the scoreboard after each score.

I recommend that you use a second camcorder on the field, near the sideline. It is his job to get some unusual pictures that might be great for a hilite tape. He should take pictures of the sideline, trainers taping, plays as they are developing, cheerleaders and even the crowd.

After each game, I will view the tape. I couldn't go to sleep anyway, so this is a perfect time to do this. I make note of any play that I think might be in a hilite tape later on. I do this by marking down the tape frame number of the VCR. I also make note of what type of play it is, so I can use this for many things later on. I can use this method for figuring our yardage on each play or making a hilite tape of the team and making a hilite tape of a particular play. Here is the way I mark each play: 007, Jones 24 Trap, +12 yds. This would mean that this play is located at frame 007 and Jones made 12 yards on the 24 Trap. If the play is hilite material, I put an asterisk in front of the play. You can see where it would be easy to throw together the plays with an asterisk. You must remember to start the tape back at "O" at the start of each tape. Obviously, it tapes 2 VCR's to copy a tape and to make a hilite tape.

The criteria for getting an asterisk by the play or to eventually be a part of the hilite tape is as follows: (1) offense=any great block, any great play, any run or pass reception over 10 yards, any great kickoff return, all touchdowns and a field goal. (2) defensively= any great tackle, any great play, any sack, anytime the runner is thrown for a loss, any pass interception, a blocked punt, any touchdown scored on defense and any great punt return.

When making the tape we will use great music. I let the kids help me pick this out. I use many graphics and animations. This year I did some morphing, where I was able to turn a player into an animal on screen. They loved this. I do a lot of scrolling of names, etc. Some plays are put in slow motion and others are funny when you speed them up. If a play is really great, I will show it a couple of times.

We try hard to keep the tape at about 30 minutes. It must be at least this long to get everything on it. If it runs over 40 minutes, you will surely lose the interest of those watching it.

We let our kids check these out from the myself or from the school library. I will also make them a copy of the tape (free), if they furnish me with a tape.

The hilite tape can be an extremely effective recruiting tool. Obviously, a player will look great if you only show his best plays. College coaches quite often don't like hilite tapes as they want to see the bad with the good. However, I've never known a college coach that would not take time to look at a hilite tape. The more tapes that you send out, the more kids you will help get some financial assistance to some college.

This year, I think our 3-A school got financial help to more of its players than any other school in the State of Iowa. We have 10 players going on to play college ball next fall. Three of them got full rides and 5 others got some kind of financial assistance.

Praise your camera person. Good camera people are hard to come by. If you have trouble getting a camera man, you can contact a college near by, as they have video classes where students are looking for ways to get some experience. Some larger high schools also have the same classes.

The main reason that I go to all the work to make a hilite tape is to get the kids pumped up for another season. They have told me that they look these over many times in the off season. Parents appreciate these too.

39. A Fair Way to Determine Letter Winners

A letter should be something that is earned and something that the athletes can be proud of. In some ways, it would be nice to give everyone a letter that participated in your sport, but if you did that it would take away the value of the letter.

At every school that I have coached at, the administration would let each coach set up his criteria for earning a letter. Surprisingly, each coach was a little different. The following requirements have worked good for me:

1. A player must end the season in good standing with the team and coaches. If they quit a week before the season was over or if they got in big trouble they would not receive a letter.

2. A player must be free of the use of alcohol.

3. A player must not chew tobacco.

4. A player must not smoke.

5. A player must be free of illegal drug usage.

6. A player must have played in approximately one/half of the quarters. If you only played in one play, you would be credited with a full quarter.

7. All seniors that finish the season in good standing will get a varsity letter.

8. A coach reserves the right to give any player a letter that has made a significant impact on the team. I like having this statement in there, because it gives you an out. You now have the right to give a letter to anyone that you want to. For example, a starter who is injured in the 4th game of the year won't have his quota of quarters in, but you could still give him a letter.

Some coaches count junior varsity quarters toward the earning of a letter. I don't agree with this, because it takes something away from the importance of a varsity letter.

Don't forget to give the manager a letter (called Manager Letter). He is an important part of your team. You should make him feel that he is really wanted.

The players that don't earn a varsity letter will be given a nice certificate. It will be called a "Participation Certificate."

I do believe in playing a lot of players and I do believe it is good to give a letter to a person who is on the border of number of quarters played. It is my experience that he will work harder in the off-season if he a letter winner. I remember in my high school days, I earned 10 letters (4 in baseball, 3 in football and 3 in basketball). I'll never forget those numbers. Kids still count the number of letters that they have earned.

It's a good idea to form a letterman's club. This is something the athletes can take pride in. It shows good "togetherness" with all of the sports. The letterman's club should put on special functions such as dances, parties and carnivals. It is another method of raising money and giving it back to the athletic program.

We have an Awards Night at the end of the season. All letters, certificates and special awards are handed out at this time. It is a memorable occasion for the athletes.

40. A Checklist of Things That Should be Included in an Awards Night

On the last night of practice we have our players vote for the following awards that will be announced on Awards Night: (1) Team captains, (2) Most Valuable Offensive Lineman, (3) Most Valuable Defensive Lineman, (4) Most Valuable Offensive Back, (5) Most Valuable Defensive Back, (6) Most Valuable Over All, and (7) any other award that they would like to see handed out on Awards Night. At the same time the coaches will also vote for some special awards such as: (1) Most Aggressive, (2) Most Coachable, (3) Best TEAM spirit, (4) Most Underrated , (5) Most Improved, and (6) any other special award that they would like handed out.

At the players last meeting, we will also hand out letters to be taken home to the parents. The letter will also contain the time and location of the Awards Night. We encourage the parents to come to Awards Night and ask them to bring a hot dish, their own plates and either a salad or dessert. Our local pizza places usually volunteer to throw in a little extra. It makes for an evening of a lot of good eating.

We usually have the Awards Night during one of the first evenings immediately after the season is over. The winter coaches don't like us to have it during their season and I don't blame them for it.

We try for a good turnout. Players are told that it is extremely important that they be there. I'm not sure which is best, whether to invite the Sophomore Team or not. I've tried both. I guess it depends on how much room you have. We also invite:

1. The cheerleaders and their sponsors.

2. All parents.

3. All of the trainers.

4. Statisticians.

5. The local Sports Writers.

6. Radio and Television personalities that had anything to do with your games.

7. Anyone else that wishes to attend.

We will advertise this by word of mouth, letters sent home to parents, in the school announcements, in the newspaper, and on the radio.

When everyone arrives, they will notice the room decorated in school colors. We will also have photos taken during the season and newspapers clippings lying around. We also play college football hilite songs as they enter. The coache's wives usually place the food in the proper place. In order to speed up things, we have 4 long rows of tables, which enables 4 different lines in getting the food.

We use to have an Invocation, but the schools can no longer allow this. I don't agree with this decision, but we have no choice but to go along with it. In section "A" we let the senior players, cheerleaders and trainers go first. Then it is the Juniors and on down to the Sophomores. In section "B" the coaches and coaches wives will go first followed by the other adults. We probably go through the line in about 10 minutes. We ask the students to take only one milk or lemonade the first time through, otherwise some of them will grab 5 or 6 of them and others will be left out.

After we eat, our program will begin. I will speak for about 7 minutes. My speech will usually consist of the following:

1. Thank everyone for coming to Awards Night and for bringing the great food.

2. Then I will introduce any special people such as assistant coaches and their wives, sport's writers, sport's announcers, team doctor, statisticians, camera man, cheerleader chaperone, etc.. I will personally thank all of them for helping us out during the season.

3. Thank everyone for their support during the season.

4. Hopefully, I'll get in a few jokes.

5. Then I will give a short summary about the season.

Now, it is time to hand out the awards. First, I introduce the cheerleader sponsor and she will introduce and say a good word about the cheerleaders. Next, I will introduce and thank the trainers for a job well done. Then I introduce the sophomore coach who will introduce and hand out his awards. He is told to keep this brief, because we would like to make sure the emphasis is placed on the seniors.

Next, we have the awards presentation to the non-letter winners. These are some very attractive "Certificates of Participation." I will then explain what it takes to earn a Varsity Letter. Then we introduce the varsity letter winners. I like to do this one at at a time trying to say something nice about them and quite often a joke about them. This is a very special moment in their lives.

Now it's time for all of the special awards that were mentioned earlier in this article. First, we hand out the awards picked by the players and then the awards chosen by the coaches. Sometimes the players will even have a gift for the coaches. This is really appreciated, but not expected.

Before the Award Night concludes, I remind the players that the coaches have prepared a "statistics" book that they may pick up. It includes team roster, photos of the players, newspapers clippings, list of award winners, and all of this year's statistics.

In conclusion, I again thank everyone for coming and making this night a memorable night for the youngsters. Remind the players to start hitting the weights hard. Also remind everyone to stick around if they want too, as I've prepared a 30 minute hilite tape. It will include the best plays of the year, as well as after game celebrations, pictures of the band, cheerleaders, crowd, practices, decorations around the town, fireworks and a lot of graphics and animation. Tell them that our Stud (Bill Jones) will turn into a pussy cat right on the screen. We do this by morphing a picture.

41. Thirty Three Tips to Take Through Time.

*TEMPTATON to join the wrong group of people can be disasterous. "Never let a bad person bring you down to their level."

*THRIVE on hard work. "Work hard and good things have a way of happening."

*TRIUMPH is just a little "Umph" added to Try.

*TARDINESS is bad. "If you can't be on time--_Be Early._"

*TEAM= **T**ogether **E**ach **A**chieves **M**ore.

*TRUST is important--so is being loyal, helpful, friendly, courteous, kind, obedient, cheerful, thrifty, brave, clean and reverent.

*TIME MANAGEMENT is significant. Be organized. "Plan your work, then work your plan." "If you fail to plan, you should plan to fail."

*TEACH yourself to _"Never give up! Never give up!"_

*TOBACCO is bad--so is Alcohol and Drugs!

*THE Ten Commandments are something we should all live by.

*TOTAL COMMITMENT should be your only way to do things.

*TRY-ON a happy face. It takes less muscles to smile than it does to frown!

*TACKLE your worst jobs early in the a.m. when you are rested and still have a clear mind.

*TEST yourself and keep educating yourself. More education will always pay dividends.

*TEARING down the opposition is not the right thing to do. Be full of Praises!

*TENACITY is a quality of all successful people.

*TERMINATE all thoughts about failure. _You can do it!_ Remember AMERICAN ends with "ICAN."

*TERRIBLE to "put down" another person. "If you don't have something good to say about someone, don't say anything."

*TREAT others like you would like to be treated.

*THERE are 2 sides to every story. Hear both sides before drawing a conclusion.

*TODAY you should praise your kids and your spouse and then do it again every day.

*TOMORROW is the worst word in the Dictionary. "Do it now" (not tomorrow)!

*TOUCH someone's life. Be a positive enfluence on their life. "You will be a better person for having made someone else a better person."

*TRACE your roots and always remember to respect those ahead of you.

*TRADITIONAL family values should always be a priority in your life!

*TRAIN yourself to always set goals. Write them down and then go-for-it.

*TRY to save money for a "rainy day." You never know when you will need it.

*TAKE care of your body. The Good Lord gave you one body. He won't give you another one. You will be living within this body your entire life. Why not make it a good place to live? You treat it good and it will treat you good!

*TRAVEL through time knowing that you have lived your life in such a way that you have no regrets.

*TAKE your time and do it right. "Inch by inch, life's a cinch--yard by yard it's hard."

*TRAGIC to think that winning is everything. It's the "_wanting to win_" that is important.

*TRIGGER your life. Have fun in whatever you are doing. Enjoy life!

*THANK the Lord _Often!_

42. What to Include in a Complete Off-Season Weight Program

If you ask 100 different weight people what the best weight program is, you'll probably get 100 different answers. There is ongoing research on this topic and it wouldn't surprise me that the recommended program will look a lot different 20 years from now. I've been in the coaching business for a long time. I've tried several different weight lifting programs and I've watched other high schools and colleges change their programs from time to time. I've formed the following beliefs:

1. The most common reason that kids do not lift weights is because they compare their strength against another person. They should never do this. There will always be someone stronger and they can make you look real weak. The person that you really want to beat is yourself.

2. Whatever program you use, keep it simple so that the athlete and all the coaches will understand it and not be confused about it.

3. It is extremely important that you stretch out before and after you lift weights.

4. Someone who understands the proper lifting techniques should be around the first few days of the program, so that the lifters don't get off on the wrong track.

5. Be extremely concerned with safety. Even the best of weight lifters are subject to injuries.

6. When setting up a program you should do quality reps. Be sure to include a program that will utilize all of the major muscle groups such as: (1) total body exercises, (2) upper and middle back, (3) shoulders, (4) arms, (5) lower back, (6) chest, (7) neck, (8) abdominals, (9) and legs. Work out at least 3 times a week.

7. I prefer 3 sets for each muscle group, as long as it is done with complete seriousness. You could do each exercise about 10 times (using about 60% of your maximum). These maximums could be increased about 5% each week. It is a good idea to test the athletes before they start the program and to test them again every 6 weeks.

8. When an athlete reaches new maximums, you could tape him doing this, so that others could see it later on. At least, note on the bulletin board any

significant achievement that this person made.

9. Free weights are much more beneficial that machine weights.

10. Have an "elite club" for any one that can bench press one and one half times his body weight. Have other awards.

11. Hand out "t-shirts" for good attendance.

43. It is Important to Support the Other Sports

It is extremely important that you support the other sports as well as all of the school activities. All activities including music, drama, organizations, publications, class leadership roles, photography, and yearbook are important in a student's life. They build character, just like athletics.

Most of your athletes will be participating in other sports and activities. They will know it when you attend these events. It means a lot to them. Do not be so one-sided as to only talk your sport with them. You'll work up a good rapport with them if you visit with them about their other activities.

You will want the support of the people involved in the other activities. If you want their support, then you better support their programs. Following are some of the things that I have done to win their support:

1. Shake their hand and wish them luck before their season begins.

2. Shake their hand to congratulate them after a good game or performance.

3. Compliment them as much as possible on the radio and television.

4. I always shake the hand of our band director before the first game and tell him that I hope that he has a good season.

5. At pep rallies, I try to compliment others. Tell the student body, the band and the cheerleaders that they are doing a great job.

6. Include the band and other groups in your hilite tape.

7. Attend the activities of others.

8. Encourage your friends to attend the other activities.

9. Help the sponsors of other activities to gain parent support.

10. If they need new facilities or equipment, help them get it.

11. Offer to help keep statistics for the other coaches.

12. Help encourage students to participate in other activities.

13. Help keep students up-beat about their activity.

Do all of the above and you will gain their support and maybe you will even be able to ask them to help you to: (1) tape games ,(2) keep statistics for you, (3) call in scores for you after the game, (4) help you obtain better equipment and facilities, (5) get a student a better grade, (6) help with the weight lifting program, (7) help encourage someone to go out for your sport, (8) scout your opponents, (9) talk your sport in the hall ways, (10) help me with impressing upon the athletes the importance of hard work and keeping a positive attitude, (11) post my announcements on the doors to their rooms, and (12) help me make sure that the students have a good outlook on life.

44. How to Have a Good Rapport With Your Athletes

To me, this is the most important thing involved in having a good football program. If you can't get along with your athletes, you are in the wrong business. It is important that you communicate properly with them both during the season and during the off season. It is important that you talk to your athletes frequently. When you see them in the hall way, talk football with them, joke with them, and find out what their interests in life are. Talk on their level. Be a good listener. They will figure out fast that you are interested in their life and well-being. This is real important to them. Praise them and encourage them and they will work harder for you. Following are some things that I do to get the kids pumped up and to have a good rapport with them:

1. We send out football newsletters to the athletes every 3 months. It contains things that have happened in our football program, such as ordering of new game uniforms, honors won by players, scholarships offered, etc.

2. Have pizza parties with the players.

3. Have fun at your practices. Have some special contests, such as 3 legged sack race. Winners get some kind of a reward.

4. Don't run sprints after practice. Do enough running during your practices while doing practical things.

5. Have family type picnics before and after the season.

6. When you see a player in the hall way tell him that you viewed the tape of the game last night and that was one heck of a tackle that you put on their tailback. I especially do this a lot in the off season, after I have viewed some of our last fall's games. The kids will get excited and want to hit the weights hard or make them more eager to get to the practice.

7. When you meet up with someone in the hall way, during the off season, tell them that you are looking forward to working with them in the fall or that you have them penciled in for a starting position.

8. Have weight room incentives. We give out t-shirts and make special notice when someone improves their maximums. We post this on a large board. We give each kid a computerized weight program.

9. Have the elementary students write the players comments during the

season.

10. We hand out a 100 page player's handbook. The kids take pride in this.

11. When someone wins a scholarship or receives an honor, make sure this is included in the school announcements.

12. We have special days that the kids look forward to, such as: watermelon, popsicle and malt days. Local business men furnish these.

13. Promote and praise the players every time that you give a talk to an organization or front of the student body, etc.

14. Have many special awards, such as scout team player, specialist award, and hardest worker of the week.

15. Play a lot of players. We believe in platooning just for this reason.

16. Periodically make motivational speeches.

17. Give the athletes several comments that they can take through life.

18. Tell the athlete how much we appreciate his efforts-- that he is a major contributing factor to our teams success.

19. Go out of your way to visit with sport's writers and sports announcers.

20. We make a year-end hilite tape that is second to none. Every player is on the tape. In fact, we have each player walk in front of the camera to introduce himself while mentioning his position and grade. All players are given a copy of the hilite tape in exchange for an empty tape.

21. We really push to get our kids some type of financial assistance to a college. This last year we had 10 boys that plan to go on and play college football. Most of them were given some type of financial assistance. I think that this is more than any other school in Iowa. It makes me feel real good and it shows me that the athletes enjoyed playing football for us.

22. After each practice we have a motivational chant given by one of our players. His name is Miller, so we call it "Miller Time." The kids like that.

23. I visit with the younger teams in the locker room or on the field after a game to give them encouragement.

24. At the end of the season, we hand out a booklet, that includes: (1) individual photos of each player, (2) award winners, (3) copies of newspapers of the games, (4) all the statistics, (5) any honors won,   (6) the team roster, and (7) the coaches rap up of the season.

25. We make handing out equipment a big thing. We play college football fight songs and we have the cheer leaders helping fill out the cards.

26. We introduce all the players at a High School Pep Rally.

27. We put emphasis on bulletin boards during the season.

28. We put (in large print) all the former athletes, from this school, that have gone on to play college football.

29. We give the athletes some say when it comes to making decisions.

30. Have the very best of equipment.

31. Have the very best of facilities.

32. If a player is a fisherman talk fishing with him. If a player is a bookworm, talk reading books with him. Talk to them on something they are interested in.

Make sure that all of your coaches help promote your program. They should talk football with athletes every time they see them. You can't do it yourself. Never let the school hire an assistant coach that does not teach in your school system. It is best if they are a member of the high school staff, but never just someone off main street.

45. Important Information on Attending Coaching Clinics

The most important thing that you have to do here is to convince the administrators and athletic director that coaching clinics are important and that you would like to have them included in your athletic budget. I've known high schools to have anywhere from $0. to $1,000 set aside for each sport. If the Administration needs convinced of this, then you should give him some evidence as what other schools in the area are doing. Do some research on this and show them proof other schools are spending a lot of money for this thing. They do not want their competition to have an unfair advantage.

After you have convinced the school to set aside a lot of money for you, set down and try to come up with the clinics that can be of the most help to you. A lot of coaches attend several clinics. I think a better thing to do is to decide what you want to emphasize next fall and then pick out a clinic that will be stressing this type of thing. For example, you plan to put in the "zone" type blocking next fall for the first time. Go to a clinic where they have a top-notch speaker on this topic. Make sure you have all of your coaches there with you. Some of the schools will only allow one or two assistants to go with you. Get this changed immediately!

I've always been one to pattern my offense and defense after a college. I guess the reason that I do this is , I once had the opportunity to an assistant coach at the University of Iowa. I was simply amazed at how intelligent an entire staff could be. They don't miss a thing. Several members of the staff that I was on went on to coach professional football. They were a special group of guys. Wayne Fontes is still the Head Coach of the Detroit Lions. I thought that I knew football until I had the opportunity to be around a great staff. Ray Nagle was our head coach. I think that Frank Gilliam, Bud Tynes, Dick Tamburo, Wayne Fontes, and Dick Tamburo all became affiliated with professional teams.

To me an ideal situation would be to take my entire staff to a clinic for 2 or 3 days at a college where they put emphasis on something that you would like to do next year. Don't get me wrong, I don't change my entire offense and defense each year, but I do like to keep up with trends in coaching. This last year I took my staff out to the Nebraska coaching clinic. I've been there before and it is an outstanding clinic. I think that they had over 800 coaches in attendance this past spring. Last year we put in the "zone" blocking principles and I wanted my coaches to see how they teach the techniques involved with "zone" blocking. Where better to go that to a watch a team that runs this type of offense 75% of the time. We want to use more man-to-man coverage in the secondary next fall and my coaches were able to watch techniques involved in man-to-man coverage. Most colleges welcome a high school staff to visit their coaching staff.

46. Things to Know About Setting Up a Schedule

Will every coach agree with me that the best way to get a football program going is to play teams that you have a reasonable chance to defeat?

Of course, a lot depends on whether you are playing in a conference, a district, or are playing independent. I have had the opportunity to coach in all 3 situations. The independent situation is the worst. The only teams that will play you are the ones that think they can defeat you and the travel time can be outrageous.

I inherited a situation once where my team was the smallest team in the conference. Other schools had 3-grade enrollments of around 1,000 and we only had 500. Before I took over the program, our school had the longest losing streak in the state (around 33 straight losses). It was a horrible situation. My first 2 years, I was only able to win 3 games each year. My kids would walk off the field crying. The community didn't care if we won or loss just as long as we had a moral victory. We changed that fast. We looked to get into a new conference, but couldn't find one. We had to go Independent for a couple of years. We were able to have winning seasons, but just barely. It was not a good situation, but it was better than getting clobbered each week. We knew that the state was about to put in district football and we were waiting for that. This would mean that the state would set up the schedules for all teams and that you would all be playing teams of equal enrollment and within a short distance. This has worked out great. At one time during the next few years, we had the states longest winning streak and the team made it to the State Playoffs several times. Again, it was obvious to me that the players enjoy winning a whole lot more than they do losing.

Even with District or Conference play, you have an opportunity to play a couple of non-district games. Again, it is best to schedule someone that you can defeat.

I think it is extremely important that you help with the schedules of the junior high, freshmen, sophomore and junior varsity teams. When I come into a new school this is the first thing that I look at. If the Junior High teams go 0 and 4, they will have no fun and will not want to go out for football come next fall. The same for all the other teams. We would all like to get our teams in a situation where they all win each year and you can think about "reloading" instead of "rebuilding." If a team goes 8 and 0, they will take a lot of pride in their work and will look forward to coming out again next fall and I'll guarantee you that a winning team will work the weights harder than a team that goes 0 and 8.

If I have a choice, we like to have our toughest games last on the schedule. Maybe, it is because we have confidence in our coaching staff.

47. Things to Know About Getting the Right Officials for Your Games

There are good officials and there are bad officials. You had better know the difference or it will cost you in the long run.

I will get a list of all of the officials in the State of Iowa. I keep a folder titled "officials." During the entire year, I write things in this folder about different things that I have learned about the officials. I get my information by way of the following:

1. I observe them at my home games and away games.

2. I talk to other coaches about the officials.

3. I study the officials on tape when I'm viewing a game of an upcoming opponent.

4. I watch them at freshmen, sophomore and junior varsity games.

5. I watch them when they are doing other sports in the off-season

6. I get a list of all of the officials that get tournament competition.

7. I go to rules meetings for coaches and officials to visit with them.

8. I talk to them on the streets.

9. I talk to them at various functions.

I know the Athletic Association would never agree with me, but I honestly think that some officials will do you a better job than others.

It is a bad idea to hire new officials. If they have never worked a high school game before, they can go practice at some other place. I don't want them. Also, the thing that I run into a lot, is that the officials group may have one new official in their group. He will be the one to really screw up things for this otherwise fine group. I grade each official. We hire only the ones with high marks and only the ones that have a lot of experience. We like the ones that work tournaments. They are usually the best.

Every coach will agree that some officials are flag happy and some officials only call the obvious penalties. It amazes me how my team can go one game with no penalties and then have 15 called on us the next game. In this day and age, an official can

135

control the outcome of a football game more than any other sport. You only get a few opportunities to score and when that official calls back a 50 yard touchdown run, it really hurts. I had one game that was played in the rain and mud. Neither team could move the ball. We had a belly series play go for a 70 yard touchdown, but the official blew an inadvertent call, because he thought the first man through had the ball. I always hire the officials who throw very little flags against both teams. If I think an official does a good job for us, we hire him back. If he does a bad job, we don't want him again. If the opponents have a bad official assigned to work our game with them at their place, we ask them to change officials, because we have a lot of trouble with them in the past. They will usually oblige us.

If you have to use a flag-happy group of officials choose them for an opponent that is heavily favored to defeat you.

48. This is a List of Good Locker Room Quotes

There is a time and place for good "motivational quotes" to be placed around the locker rooms and hall ways. With the new modern technology, you can really make some attractive posters. Current computer programs allow you to make posters with some outstanding graphics. I post them year around to keep the athletes pumped up on the sport that I'm coaching. Ask your athletes to come up with some slogans for you. You'll be surprised with what they come up with. Following are my favorite quotes:

1. "You are the only one who can use your ability. It is an awesome re sponsibility."

2. "Smile and the world smiles with you, cry and you cry alone."

3. "American ends with ICAN."

4. "The more you thank God for what you have--the more you will have to thank God for."

5. "When your image improves, your performance improves."

6. "If you learn from a defeat, you haven't really lost."

7. "When the going gets tough, the tough get going."

8. "A winner never quits, a quitter never wins."

9. "You're not beaten by being knocked down. You're only beaten if you stay down."

10. "Luck is what happens, when preparation meets opportunity."

11. "He can, who thinks he can."

12. "The will to win, will win."

13. "No one on the face of this earth can make you feel inferior without your per- mission.

14. "We should be thankful for our tears: they prepare us for a clearer vision of god."

15. "You can count on me."

16. "Attitude is everything."

17. "Smiles are contagious."

18. "If you want a friend, be a friend."

19. T.E.A.M means Together Everyone Achieves More."

20. "Think big!"

21. "Motivation is a fire from within. If someone else tries to light that fire under you, chances are it will burn very briefly."

22. "To have something to achieve, and then to do it, is the secret to success."

23. "There is no 'I' in TEAM."

24. "When contentment enters, progress ceases."

25. "Every great feat is at first impossible."

26. "Work hard and good things have a way of happening."

27. "What the winner has that the loser hasn't---confidence."

28. "All wish to possess greatness, but few are willing to pay the price."

29. "Defeat is for those who acknowledge it."

30. "Winning isn't everything, but it sure beats coming in second."

31. "The greater the difficulty, the more glory in surmounting it."

32. "It is easy to avoid criticism--say nothing, do nothing and be nothing."

33. "Knowledge has to be improved, challenged, and increased constantly or it vanishes."

A couple of the above quotes may be religious and might offend some people. If this is the case, I would not post those.

49. Current Trends in Modern Technology That Can Benefit a Coach

It's amazing how things have changed during my years of coaching. In the 1950s we did not have camcorders. Instead, we would use movie cameras and the processed film of the game would cost around $100. Many times we would have to wait 3 days before we got it developed. We didn't have ear phones. We would yell back and forth from the press box. We didn't have computers to figure statistics, etc. Of course, we didn't have VCR's, editing machines, and digitized scouting.

A good VHS camcorder should be your first investment. Get one that has a color viewer and has a zoom capability of at least 12 to 1, but preferably 24 to 1. Most camcorders cost between $400 to $900. However, there is a trend to purchase super-VHS camcorders. These cameras cost from $2,000 to $4,000. The quality of the picture is much better. I've never been at a school that had a S-VHS, but I have seen tapes from other schools that had them. Colleges and professionals use them a lot. If you purchase a S-VHS camcorder, you must make sure that your VCR and Monitor are compatible. Be sure to get a camera that has several special effects as you can use these effects for a Hilite tape at the end of the season.

Along with a good camcorder, you need a good method of projecting the game tape to a large screen. You can do this several ways, but to me the simplest thing to do, is to just purchase a 50 inch television set for about $2000. Other projectors cost this much but they lose the advantage of having a television set around for other things. For example, our team will quite often set around and watch the big rivalry of Iowa vs. Iowa State.

You need at least 2 VCR's to copy tapes. I own about 5 VCR's at my home and it seems like they are constantly in use. VCR's cost any where from $150. to $400. Again, it is a good idea to get at least one of them that possesses special effects. They now have editing machines that you can copy and edit games. These are great to have, but they are expensive. I've seen editing machines (with no monitors) for under $1,000 and I've seen editing machines (with 2 monitors) up to a cost of $10,000.

There are some tremendous digital scouting programs out there. With a push of a finger you can bring up any tendency that the opponents might have. Most of these programs are available for a cost of about $100.

All schools now have computers. Make sure the school gives you a good one, with a lot of memory on it. I use my computer for making rosters, equipment inventories, scouting tendencies, making transparencies for the over head projector, football posters, statistics, locker room slogans, football newsletters, and hilite tapes. I can also do morphing where I can take a person and turn him into an animal. The kids see this in the hilite tape and they really laugh over this. Join the internet, it is a great place to communicate with other coaches. I use internet to get all kinds of information about trends on offense and defense. You can purchase all kinds of programs related to football. I use many of the graphics on the computer and post things around the locker room. Most of my slogans are made with graphics. Below, is a sample of one graphic that I have used:

"I'll be DOG-GONE, the Boone Toreadors made it to the State Playoffs again!"

50. It's Great to be a Coach

I owe coaching and athletics a lot. They have been extremely good to me. I'm forever thankful that my parents encouraged me to participate in athletics when I was at a young age. I am from a family of 10 children. My parents are Clarence and Dorothy Tryon of Glidden, Iowa. My dad and my older brother, Ray, have passed on now. For a period of 30 straight years there was a Tryon participating (in some capacity) on a Glidden High School Athletic Team. We all had a strong love for athletics; 9 of the 10 children ended up being teachers. The 7 boys (Bill, Dale, Gaylord, Larry, Jerry, Dick and Randy) all did some coaching and both of my sisters (Donna and Nancy) married coaches. I've often wondered if there is another family in the country that has 9 brothers or sisters that all teach? I wonder if there are 7 brothers from one family that have coached? By coincidence, 5 of the brothers coached at an Iowa High School that was located on Highway 30 (the Lincoln Highway).

Of course, we have had to coach against each others several times. None of us liked to do this, as it was always a no win situation. After one game where my team defeated my brother's team, my dad asked all the boys to come in and paint his home the next day. My brother and I got along fine. He painted on one side of the house and I painted on the other. Later, however, we always seem to get things worked out. Now we look back at those times and laugh together. I really am proud of my family. They've all worked hard to make something of themselves. They are excellent teachers and coaches in my book. My parents were selected as BV College Parents of the year back in the 1970's. I think 5 of the brothers were selected as BV College Graduate Coach of the Year.

I'm sure many of my coaching philosophies were instilled into me at an early age. I certainly learned from my brothers what it meant to be **competitive**. The Tryon boys would go 2 against 2 or 3 against 3 in all types of activities. One of my favorites was playing basketball outside. We would nail a wood box (bottom open) to a tree and we would use rolled up socks or a tin can for the basketball. We had no rules. Everything was legal. You never saw so much pushing and shoving. One time I got so mad that I hit my brother (behind the head) with a tin can. This is when I learned the importance of **team work**, because if I got in a fight, I would need a team mate (brother) to help me out. We even played this silly game on the ice in the winter time.

Through the years the Tryon family has put on what they called the "super-star competition." We would pick out activities that everyone could do. Even the folks who were in their late 70's would compete. Some of the activities were:

1. checkers

2. horseshoes

3. one mile run

4. hitting a ball for distance

5. shot put

6. free throw shooting contest

7. scrabble

8. croquet

9. tennis

You could pick out any 5 events and scores would be posted throughout the day. It was a great event. There must have been at least 35 entrants, including Clarence and Dorothy Tryon, their 10 sons and daughters and a whole slug of grandsons and granddaughters. There were a lot of good athletes in the group. I figured that there were approximately a dozen that had made an all-state team. One year the Des Moines Register, Iowa's largest newspaper, picked up on this story and came to the little town of Glidden Iowa to witness it and later did a feature article on it.

THE TRYON'S, Front row L to R, Dale, Clarence, Dorothy and Ray. Second Row L to R, Gaylord, Donna, Bill and Nancy. In the Back Row L to R, Randy, Larry, Jerry and Dick.

I'm not sure why we all got into coaching, but I know how I did. When I graduated from high school, I wasn't sure what I wanted to do for a profession. All I knew was that I wanted to go on to College to participate in athletics. My older brother, Bill, was attending Buena Vista College as a senior, and I wanted the chance to play on the same team with him, so I went up north 60 miles to BV. I couldn't afford to purchase books, so I just used the same ones that my older brother used. After 4 years, they told me that I had a degree and that I could now coach and teach. This is pretty close to how it all happened.

I started out as a Junior High Coach at Manson High School and after 2 years was given the opportunity to be the Head Coach at Manson High. After several years I moved on to coach at Audubon, then to Cedar Rapids Kennedy and then served on Ray Nagel's staff at the University of Iowa. I left coaching for a few years to give the world of business a try. I soon found that I really missed the excitement of coaching. I got back to coaching at Ames High School and then on over to Boone High School. I love the profession and I hope I am able to stay in it for a long time.

I have no idea what my won-loss record is. It really isn't that important to me. I know that I've won somewhere between 70 and 85% of my games. I know that during 5 decades of coaching, my teams have won their respective conference or district titles approximately one-half of the time. The main thing to me is whether or not the athlete is a better person for having gone out for football. I think the administrators and school boards should consider the above rather than the won-loss record of a coach, when it comes to hiring and firing. I've known a lot of great coaches that didn't win many games, but they were in a "graveyard" situation with no material. I've also know some very poor coaches that have won a lot of games, but they were blessed with having a lot of talent or located at the largest school in the conference.

I knew early on that I wanted to work with young kids. Some of my early coaches were a big influence on my life. My high school coaches, Jim Crimmings, Dick Nystuen and Ray Byrnes were great with working with us. In college, I had great respect for Coach Jay Beckman. I could see how they inspired and motivated us and I thought I wanted to be just like them. I wanted to be able to touch someone's life. I wanted to be a positive influence on someone's future. I wanted to make a difference in their life.

One of the biggest pleasures of coaching is watching the athletes develop physically and mentally. I especially admire the ones that really worked for everything that they got. I think of my 4 children: (1) Danny, was my oldest boy, he started out not very strong and wasn't very big. He wanted to be a quarterback, but his hands were too small to grasp a football. They pushed him aside until his senior year and they finally gave him a chance. Because he had worked hard on weights, passing, agility drills, etc., through the years he was beginning to develop. By the time the year was over he had the best passing records of any quarterback in the conference, which was thought to be the best conference in the state of Iowa. (2) My next son, Donnie, never started until he was a senior year. Again he was pushed aside at a younger age, but I

143

encouraged him to stick with it. He worked at it and as a senior he led the same conference in pass receptions. (3) My youngest son, David got 50th out of 55 junior high students in a physical fitness test of all football players. It consisted of weight lifting, sprint running and distance running. No one worked harder than he did. In his senior year, he took the same test with the same kids and was 3rd to the best. He was an outstanding defensive end on a State Playoff Team. (4) My only girl, Jodie, came along when girl's athletics were just being put into the schools. Because of her hard work she was a contributing factor for the success of her basketball team and track team. She also worked hard enough to be a 4.0 student. Ironically, none of my children ever started a junior high game. It just goes to show you to never give up on any youngster, because those that are hard workers will make it in time. Everyone measures height, weight and strength but they fail to measure the heart. I'm sure my wife, Janet, will agree with me that that our children got a lot out of participating in athletics. Their lives were molded during this time. They now understand the importance of hard work, getting up after being knocked down, that failure is only temporary, the meaning of discipline, setting goals, organization, team work, sportsmanship, attitude, and leadership.

THE TRYON'S: First row, L to R, Dale, daughter Jodie, and Janet. Back row, L to R, Doug Stokke (Jodie's husband) and son's Danny, David and Donnie.

There are a lot of other good things about teaching: (1) June, July and August. (2) you have time to do other money making things, (3) an opportunity to build character, and (4) a chance to meet a lot of great people in this profession.

To me, one of the biggest satisfactions that I get from coaching is when a former player comes back to me and says, "Coach, I learned a lot from you. You were a role model for me. You have made my life easier. I'm using a lot of things in life that I learned from you. I'm a better person for having the opportunity to play for you." That's what coaching is all about!

Obviously, not all things are rosy in coaching. You will need to work long hard hours. You just need to make the long hours seem fun to you. **"We do not stop working and playing because we grow old, we grow old because we stop working and playing."** Sometimes you are going to fail. You don't always win! I've always ʼ **"If you are afraid of failing, get out of the business."** Also, you are going criticized. It's just part of the profession. Accept it! **"It is easy to avoid :ism, say nothing, do nothing, and you will be nothing.**

nk God for giving me the opportunity to be able to work with America's youth. people get up in the morning and say **"Good-God Morning?"**. They hate their ssion and don't look forward to going to work. I wake up in the morning nstead of saying **"Good-God Morning,"** I say **"Good Morning God."** I've now hed during 5 decades. I feel good in what I've done. Coaching has been good to -I hope I've been good to coaching. It's the greatest profession in the world. I sider myself one of the luckiest people on the face of the earth.